THE BARLINNIE STORY

Also by Robert Jeffrey

Gentle Johnny Ramensky
A Boxing Dynasty (with Tommy Gilmour)
Real Hard Cases (with Les Brown)
Crimes Past
Glasgow Crimefighter (with Les Brown)
Glasgow's Godfather
Gangs of Glasgow (first published as *Gangland Glasgow*)
Glasgow's Hard Men
Blood on the Streets
The Wee Book of Glasgow
The Wee Book of the Clyde

*

Clydeside People and Places
The Herald Book of the Clyde
Doon the Watter
Images of Glasgow
Scotland's Sporting Heroes (with Ian Watson)

THE BARLINNIE STORY

RIOTS, DEATH, RETRIBUTION AND REDEMPTION
IN SCOTLAND'S INFAMOUS PRISON

ROBERT JEFFREY

BLACK & WHITE PUBLISHING

First published 2009
This edition first published 2011
by Black & White Publishing Ltd
29 Ocean Drive, Edinburgh EH6 6JL

3 5 7 9 10 8 6 4   13

ISBN: 978 1 84502 334 8

Typeset by Ellipsis Books Limited, Glasgow
Printed and bound by Nørhaven, Denmark

CONTENTS

I would like to thank the friendly and efficient staff of the Glasgow Room in the Mitchell Library for their help in the production of this book. Also Bill McKinlay, former Governor of Barlinnie, his secretary Jane O'Brien, current Governor Derek McGill, Ron Ferguson, Dr Grant Jeffrey and a legion of lawyers, lawbreakers, prison officers and policemen.

RJ
Carradale, Argyll

To the men and women of the Scottish Prison Service

INTRODUCTION

Iconic. That is the word for Barlinnie, Scotland's largest jail, aka the Bar-L. The former Governor, Bill McKinlay, jocularly reckons that worldwide the name is better known than Edinburgh Castle. Though let there be no doubt that Barlinnie is no tourist attraction despite the huge numbers of repeat visitors. This massive sandstone edifice, in the east end of Glasgow, was opened in 1882 and the newspapers of the time remarked on the light colour of the stone it was built from, which was said to shine in the summer sun.

Over the years the stone has turned to a grimy black and the sunshine of hope that saw the massive building project as a solution to overcrowding in Glasgow's Victorian prisons has withered. Barlinnie has been, almost from the moment it opened, overcrowded. It is still in 2011 clearly, in the phrase of the day, not fit for purpose. In particular because that purpose is much more than incarceration. 'We are not here,' said Bill McKinlay, 'just to take people's freedom away. We're here to be facilitators and to allow people to change.' Those, that is, who have the will to change.

Bill McKinlay is a vastly experienced member of the prison service. Everything he knows from his long service in all sorts of jails and in many different roles underlines his belief that HMP Barlinnie should be blitzed by the wrecker's ball and a new start made in Glasgow in a new prison. He is not the first to think that way and he is not alone. He acknowledges that

1

there are those who argue that these sandstone monoliths must still be useful if for no other reason than they are still standing. 'Well, so are the pyramids. But no one has been buried inside them for some time,' former Governor McKinlay points out wryly.

In the ongoing Barlinnie story thousands have been buried, and are continuing to be buried, in the great, echoing halls. Cast out from society, sentenced to pay for their crimes in one of the toughest, most infamous prisons in the world. Alcatraz, the Bangkok Hilton, Folsom, Strangeways, Pentridge, the Scrubs . . . Barlinnie has an infamous place high in the list of the world's most fearsome jails. And still, day after day, the buses – now owned by a private company – ferry the guilty from some of the busiest courts in the world through the crowded streets of Glasgow to begin their time. But it's no consolation to those who are in a living hell that they are part of the ongoing history of one of the world's iconic prisons.

That history is a strange mixture of villainy, humanity, tragedy, drama and hope. The hope is that the future for this grim place, and those incarcerated in it, will improve. That somehow the hope of the Victorians who built it will turn to reality, the hope that redemption will finally triumph over revenge. There is, however, no great grounds for optimism since for most of its 120 or so years of life Barlinnie has been a permanently over-crowded and, until as recently as 2002 when slopping out ended, an unsanitary repository for thousands of lawbreakers. If hope is a contentious issue, the drama surrounding Barlinnie is unde-niable. Down the years the prison has sparked thousands of headlines. Drama and danger go with the job, as those in the prison service who are charged by society to look after the villains know only too well.

This Barlinnie Story is not a formal or indeed a chronological history of the prison it is an unofficial, perhaps sometimes idio-syncratic, attempt to chronicle some of the momentous events in the long turbulent life of an establishment that is infamous worldwide. And an attempt to let ordinary Glaswegians, who have never darkened the doors of any prison and are never likely to, get a taste of what life was like down the years for prison officers who fostered their careers in the 'Big Hoose' in the east end, as well as for the men who festered there, sometimes taking the short walk from the condemned cell to the gallows.

There is no shortage of drama – escapes, hangings, unrest, political prisoners, a groundbreaking and visionary experiment in prison reform, humanity and brutality. All these are part of the story and the history of Barlinnie.

1

FLYING SLATES, BURNING MATTRESSES AND HOSTAGE HELL

The happenings in the east end of Glasgow one week in January 1987 were as spectacular as anything seen in the jail since it opened its doors to the city's villains in the 1880s. Many insiders, and those who had read the Prison Inspectorate's reports with diligence, were not surprised at the violent outbreak of disorder. They had seen it coming. But one of the officers who was on the front line in the chaotic battle to secure the prison told me that he and his colleagues were not ready for the scale of what happened. In fact most of those who had read the warning signs were taken aback by the enormity of the '87 riot – the longest lasting siege in the history of Scottish prisons.

When the pressure pot that was Barlinnie finally blew its top, the confrontation between prisoners and staff was violent, dangerous and potentially deadly. The newspapers broke the story on the morning of Tuesday, 6 January 1987, though anyone in the vicinity of the prison on the Monday could have seen the drama first hand as cons on the roof threw slates at the prison officers. Even concrete blocks prised from the floors were dropped on officers in riot gear by prisoners who had wrecked large areas of the jail and smashed their way into the pharmacy in search of drugs.

5

Inevitably the early reports were confused as to exactly when the riot started and what was really going on behind those high, thick walls of age-blackened sandstone. For five dark, cold midwinter days the story unfolded in a hotchpotch of lurid headlines, speculation, leader articles, features and spectacular pictures. It was big news worldwide. The press and television had a field day – this was a prison riot on their doorsteps, as spectacular as anything Hollywood could dream up, a potential life and death struggle between some of the hardest men in Scotland and their jailors.

It was a fairly hysterical few days as the press reported – or sometime guessed at – the twists and turns in the drama, day by day. Illustrative of the intensity of the media coverage was the fact that after a helicopter and film crew had flown over Barlinnie, the Scottish Office successfully applied to the Civil Aviation Authority for a ban on flights over the prison. They claimed the flights were interrupting negotiations. Aye, right, as they say in Glasgow. A more serious matter was the news the prisoners were getting from the radio on the progress of the riot and at one stage Radio Clyde and BBC Radio Scotland imposed a seven-hour news blackout as it was believed the airing of too much detail could hamper talks between the two warring sides, then at a delicate stage.

A measure of the press hysteria was the number of bylines on the stories coming out in the papers day after day during the siege. In the eighties it had become quite normal for such as the *Daily Express* and *Daily Record* to run major news stories with anything up to ten reporters bylined. On occasion they even used the phrase *Record* or *Express* 'team' at the top of the story and at the end of the tale a list of those involved in compiling it was given. This was in the days when news desks still had bundles of money to throw at the coverage of a big story, the golden days before TV became king of news coverage. For the Barlinnie riot even the douce old *Herald* (then the *Glasgow Herald*) had a double byline on the first reports from the prison, the reporters, long time stalwarts Auslan Cramb and Maurice Smith, both major players in *Herald* history. But later in the week the broadsheets, even the broadsheet *Herald*, succumbed to the multiple byline as the story grew ever important. Other legendary *Herald* men like Barclay McBain, John Easton, Bill McDowall and Andy McCallum were soon enjoying their bylines at the top of the dozens of stories in the paper each day featuring the riot. This was the BIG story.

In these days the *Herald* had a rather distant, superior attitude to its rivals. I remember from my days on the paper that the prevalent attitude was not to worry about missing a story, you just ran it the day after the tabloids, after all nothing *really* happened till the *Herald* printed it! Or so some who had been with the paper a tad too long thought. A remarkable little insight into this attitude came about when the first sputnik was launched. The newspapers of the day reacted as if little green men had landed on Earth. The *Herald* took it calmly, dismissing early wire stories as 'unconfirmed reports' and catching up on the historic event in leisurely fashion the next day.

Incidentally the *Record* was, and probably still is, the paper of choice for the inmates though these days the *Sun* runs it close. Their faith in it was solid and not just based on the tales of the Old Firm, Celtic and Rangers, that covered the sports pages. Respect is a great word much in use by lawbreakers and the tabloid had earned the respect of the criminal classes, no doubt due to the space it gave to cover the constant Glasgow crime war between the gangs and the cops. And the in-depth knowledge the paper's news desk and reporters had on the goings-on of the bad guys. This respect was so strong that a

Record man had been called to help the authorities in the negotiations at riots at Saughton and Peterhead the year before the
Barlinnie siege. In the late eighties the prison service was close
to anarchy. In the '87 Bar-L siege the prisoners shouted from
the roof to the crowds below that they wanted to speak to a
Record man. It didn't happen. This was an era of trouble in
most of Scotland's penal institutions and the press guys were
deployed with regularity to the country's prisons. So much so
that some of the reporters who had covered the other riots now
gave serious thought to producing a T-shirt with the slogan:
Scottish Prison Tour 86–87 – Saughton, Peterhead and Barlinnie.
But in reality there was little to be humorous about.

The Peterhead riot was a major incident and one prison officer,
John Crossan, was held hostage along with more than 40 inmates
by a group of three prisoners. This siege in the prison up on
the cold north-east coast, which lasted for four days, created a
Scottish prison record for such an event though a few months
later the undesirable record for the longest siege passed to
Barlinnie. The riot in P-head, as the prisoners call it, ended in
a blaze that caused half a million pounds of damage. Talking
to Barlinnie staff who had been involved in the five-day siege
they wondered if, looking back, a desire to break the record
was a factor in prolonging the disturbance. Certainly, once the
record was broken, the Barlinnie riot collapsed pretty quickly.

The Peterhead happenings had come less than a fortnight
after a three-day siege at Saughton in Edinburgh when five
men held a prison officer at knifepoint before giving themselves up. The trouble at these two establishments had been
put down to alleged brutality against the inmates. And the
same accusation was to become central to the investigation of
the trouble in the Bar-L. All the media hullabaloo round the
'87 riot meant that a clear and concise picture of what really

happened would take years to emerge. The calm legal language used in the HM Inspector of Prisons' report of 1990 was as cool as some of the newspaper reports of the 'incident', as the authorities liked to call it, was overwrought. It stated the facts: 'On 5 January 1987, following a number of seemingly unrelated incidents during the day, a major incident began in B-Hall [holding convicted prisoners] at 19.35 hours which was not resolved till the morning of 10 January. During the incident massive damage was done to the hall; staff were trapped in cells and other areas; fires were started to try to burn staff out of cells; and five staff were taken hostage. In the event, two of the hostages were freed or freed themselves within a very short time, and the others were released on the 8th and 9th of January respectively. The incident concluded with the surrender of a core group of 12 inmates at 09.28 on 10 January.'

Surrender – a lovely word for the authorities to use! But for a few days it looked more like 'no surrender' as convicts in balaclavas or improvised hoods with eyeholes cut into them, sometimes made from blackened pillowcases, roamed the roof tossing down slates to the great danger of anyone on the ground. The rioters had control over the top floor of B-Hall, hence the easy access to the tiles. They shouted and screamed abuse at their jailers, the world in general and the then Governor Andrew Gallacher in particular. They also hung sheets over the walls and between the chimneys with slogans like 'Slasher Gallagher' and 'brutality'.

The early stories in the *Herald* were calm, as you would expect, and it took a day or two for Scotland's leading broadsheet to work up to the full fury expressed by its tabloid rivals, though when it did so it did it powerfully, including a particularly long leader, even for the *Herald*, analyzing why the Scottish prison system was in the state it was in. But the first words were matter of fact. On 6 January the lead story began: 'Rioting prisoners threw slates from the roof of Barlinnie prison, Glasgow, early today and made allegations of brutality at the jail. One prison officer was injured after trouble broke out at B-Hall and up to 20 inmates were said to be involved. At one point seven men, two of them masked, could be seen on the roof. One claimed to be a hostage. The trouble is believed to have started at 8pm after a day of minor incidents.'

There are a couple of skewed details in this early report: the trouble had started nearly 12 hours earlier than suggested and the incidents were far from minor.

The report went on: 'A group of prisoners on the top floor of B-Hall later threw missiles at prison officers. When the wardens retreated, the group barricaded itself on the top floor. Some made their way to the roof.' The Scottish Office press team was about to start one of the busiest weeks in their history and they started with a predictably negative statement that seemed to run in the face of the facts. They denied that any hostages had been taken, though one of the men on the roof said he was being held against his will and that he had just four weeks of his sentence to serve. Another protester shouted down from the roof that hostages were being held inside the hall.

The next day the picture of what was happening inside the prison became clearer. By now there was talk of three officers being held hostage. The seriousness of what was going on could not be played down by the Scottish Office or the prison authorities and as darkness fell one of the hostages was paraded on the roof of B-Hall. A homemade knife was held at his throat and he screamed, 'They are going to kill me.' Maybe it was something to do with the bitter cold of a January night in Glasgow but, in any case as the light faded, the prisoners claimed from the roof, shouting to the throng of pressmen and police below, that they had reached an agreement with the authorities that there would be no more violence that night.

The Scottish Office then named the three men held: David Flanagan, 28; Andrew Smith, 23; and John Kearney, 40. It was said negotiations for their release were being conducted with the inmates who had earlier trapped 41 officers on the top floor of B-Hall. Their bosses said all three men were married and were 'experienced' officers. These three and two others had barricaded themselves in a cell on the third floor of the hall to escape the violence of the disturbance on the first night. But the prisoners had broken into the cell and grabbed them, though the other two were released unharmed. The Scottish Office was now briefing the press in some detail and after the 'peace pledge' of the second night they announced that 120 of the 188 long- and short-term prisoners in B-Hall had left it. Many of remaining prisoners were out of their cells milling about and were given tea and sandwiches.

The leaders of the group involved in the hostage situation, about 24 strong, claimed, 'the prison officers have backed out and there will be no violence from the prisoners. Agreement has been reached on this. This is a peaceful protest but we are prepared to stay here until our demands are met. We would like to reiterate that the prison officers are being kept in good conditions, the best we can give them.' The rooftop spokesman then shouted to reporters that the officers wanted messages passed to their families saying they were all right. It was a frightening, sinister and surreal scene with the prisoners masked and wearing bed sheets as cloaks. The spokesman then calmly told the reporters, 'It has been a long day for all of us and you must be cold. I would like to say that is all for tonight. We will be out again at dawn.'

This bizarre press conference had been preceded by a sortie by prison officers into the hall that helped free 27 of the 41 trapped, but it was no soft touch – flying slates, bottles and other makeshift weapons injured 34 of the officers. Three were so severely hurt they had to go to the Royal Infirmary, one man with a broken ankle and others with cuts and bruises. Detectives had been dispatched to the Royal to interview the injured and the police had also set up an incident room at Baird Street police station to collate information on what was going on at the prison.

The situation inside the prison in the early days was almost impossible for anyone on the outside to visualise. Today Dale Elliot is First Line Manager in the prison, a pleasant, humorous, fit looking man in a crisp white shirt, proud of the two 'pips' on his shoulders, sitting in his office in front of the inevitable computer, competently answering telephone queries from his staff. Back in 1987 he was a prison officer with just a few years' experience. Nothing had prepared him for what was to happen that week in the jail. Some say the trouble had been brewing for months, which may be the case, but Dale says the officers there on the day were truly taken by surprise by the riot. And even now no one can pinpoint with certainty what exactly started the mass violence, though there are theories galore. It came like a lightning strike out of a clear sky. Though inside the dark world of Barlinnie you don't see too much of that. In these days there was little contingency planning and training for an outbreak of violence such as happened that bitterly cold week in January.

The first Dale heard of what was going on in the prison and on the roof was in a late-night phone call to his home and on the first morning he was there at five along with fellow officers from Barlinnie and elsewhere. He was to be on duty in this major emergency for many long, dangerous hours. What Dale saw on entering B-Hall was a nightmare – rubbish and debris piled up on the stairs, blocking access to the top floor where the hard core of the rioters was holed up. Stones, slates, woodwork, mattresses – anything the prisoners could lay their hands on was hurled on to the stairs. The warders were marshalled much of the time by a well known and highly experienced Barlinnie officer, Bob Mutch, who, with other senior officers, was trying to create some sense of order in a nightmare environment.

Working to try and clear this mess was dangerous as well as arduous. The scene was chaotic and confused. Makeshift missiles flew about the heads of the warders. 'It was,' says Dale, 'a miracle that no one was killed,' though plenty of blood did flow. 'Brave,' says Dale, is the only adjective for the guys who were trying to restore order. Their stamina was also tested – many stayed in the jail for up to 56 hours without a break. At home their families waited and wondered though Dale says there was a great support network with wives of warders looking out for themselves and each other, starved of real news about what was going on. But they knew the danger that faced their guys in the front line.

Even in the midst of all this there was a touch of prison humour. Dale recalls that the rioters holding the hostages gorged on crisps, Mars bars and juice looted from the prison supplies. Naturally the pharmacy and the canteen had been early targets for the rioters. However, as later reports confirmed, the hostages were not too brutally treated though a rioter gave a tough warning to one: 'Stop eating all our Mars bars or we will give you back!'

While all this was going on in B-Hall the staff were trying to maintain some normality in the rest of the prison. Dale remembers, rather surprisingly, that in that perverse way of Scots, many of the prisoners in the other great halls who were not involved in the riots but were aware of what was going on, were almost on their best behaviour, showing some solidarity with the warders.

One tale underlines the fact that even at the height of the riot and afterwards some inmates did not share the feeling of the mob who were hanging sheets from the rooftop with 'Slasher Gallacher' emblazoned on them. Not long after the riot was over there was a prison concert and a skit in which one of the cons appeared dressed up as Governor Andrew Gallacher. The audience rewarded this appearance with a deadly silence, but the so-called 'Slasher' Gallacher, every eye on him, simply burst out laughing. And so then did the audience.

There had been violent mood swings from the protesters in the early days of the protest. After the so-called peace pledge for the night made at that bizarre press conference, fire hoses had been trained on the roof but they were switched off swiftly when shouts from the roof claimed, 'Guys are going to be fucked about if you don't turn the water off.' The authorities did so and claimed the hoses had only been intended to flush loose slates and debris off the roof.

Tempers and emotions were running high. A humane side to the protest surfaced briefly with the release of a prison officer who was a diabetic and urgently needed insulin. In contrast, the bright lights turned on the protestors angered them to the point that the press corps was showered with stones and slates, one hitting *Herald* photographer Arthur Kinloch. But the reason behind the riot was now slowly beginning to emerge. During the day the prisoners' spokesman repeated allegations about brutality in the prison system. This theme was echoed in the three banners that were hanging from the upper parts of B-Hall. One read, in a reference to the governor, 'Gallagher is brutality'; a second read 'To the death' and the third said 'Sammy Ralston was tortured.' Ralston, nicknamed 'The Bear' and a long-time thorn in the flesh of the prison authorities, was convicted on a robbery charge and was serving six years. He had previously staged a solo rooftop protest in November '86 while on remand on the robbery charge. The protestors claimed that he had been beaten with sticks and gagged to muffle his screams. Ralston's mother travelled to the jail to see him, convinced that if he was alright, 'I could tell the boys on the roof'. She was not allowed to do so.

Whatever the truth about the treatment of Ralston it was now the turn of the prison staff to suffer a form of torture. During the second day of the siege, prisoners had set fire to a mattress and yelled that they had trapped prison staff behind the blaze. It was chilling stuff: 'We had them screaming for mercy. We gave them it. We put out the fire. We won't do it next time.' The rioters then brought a succession of riot shields, batons and a riot helmets through the hole they had knocked in the roof and held them up as trophies. This was no doubt an attempt to convince the press that they had 'won' the equipment in a battle with the staff. The authorities thought the trophies more likely came from a storeroom in B-Hall.

Rather ironically the Scottish Home Affairs minister, Ian Lang, had been due to visit the prison that day but urgent government business took him elsewhere. However he went on TV to say that any prisoner alleging brutality could have complaints investigated by the police or the procurator fiscal, acting independently of the prison service. He also defended the prison service's record and said a lot was being done to rehabilitate prisoners. He also played down the stories of overcrowding in comments that seemed to fly in the face of the facts. On the brutality allegations, the secretary of the Scottish Prison Officers'

Association, John Renton, said: 'I ask you to consider this. Thirty-four of my members have been injured. I have heard no reports of prisoners being hurt. It's nonsense.' So ended the second day.

The *Herald* had now decided that the trouble at the Bar-L (and Peterhead and Saughton before it) was now grave enough to earn what the paper's staff called 'a long leader'. It was a good one that did not miss the mark. Ian Lang was not alone in pointing out that prisoners could complain to the police or the procurator fiscal. The then director of the Scottish Prison Service, Alistair Thompson, had made similar remarks at the time of the Saughton and Peterhead incidents. To describe such remarks 'as ingenuous would be charitable', thundered the paper. The paper wanted reforms aimed not at just suppressing the recurrent violence but removing its causes. Good sound sense. To do this, it pointed out, would be very much in the interests not just of the prisoners but also of the prison officers and the public, 'which pays £200 a week for each of the 5,000 prisoners in Scottish jails.'

On 8 January, three days after the start of the saga, it took a sinister twist – fire raising. Not this time in the prison but at the home of an officer who had been involved in the Peterhead siege, John Crossan. He lived just a couple of miles from Barlinnie in Haghill. Mr Crossan, his brother and his parents had a lucky escape. His mother smelled smoke seeping into the flat and called the fire brigade. Officers using breathing equipment rescued the family and neighbours across the landing. It all highlighted the dangers, on and off duty, faced by prison officers. Tempers were running high in the under-world as each day the papers and television showed the dramatic scenes of the rooftop siege. John Crossan, who himself had been held hostage in the Peterhead siege, found time to sympathise, in the midst of his family's plight, with that of the Barlinnie hostages. 'I feel for them because I know what they are going through. I can only pray that they get out all right.'

Back at the prison the authorities moved to cut off the inmates' contacts with the outside world in an attempt to break the deadlock. By now 26 inmates were holding three officers hostage. The flocks of journalists covering the story from the doorstep of the prison were moved out of shouting range, 300 yards or so down the road from the prison entrance. Visits to prisoners and hostages were stopped. Earlier there had been emotional scenes when the wife of a protesting prisoner had turned up outside the prison walls complete with baby in pushchair. It was the sort of touch you might have expected in a Victorian melodrama, not during a potentially deadly siege. 'You are only making it worse for yourself. Please come down. Ronnie, I love you,' she shouted through tears to her husband. 'You are going to get hell. Think of the weans.'

Her husband shouted back from the roof: 'Don't worry about me. I will be all right. Worry about the weans.' He then announced to all and sundry that his was an individual protest, he was not with the mass of the rioters, and that he had been the victim of a police 'fit up', not a unique claim in Barlinnie. His wife was led away in tears but returned later in a second failed attempt to talk her husband down. The *Sun*, always quick with memorable headlines, labelled their story on this touching little scene – 'Come doon, Ron, Ron, Ron'!

A more cerebral comment on this episode in the riot came more than ten years later in a first-class little book by Ewan McVicar (published by Glasgow City Libraries) entitled *One Singer One Song*, a collection of Glasgow folk songs. The writers of 'Screw's Barlinnie Blues' were Jim McKenna, what the habitués of folk clubs call a floor singer, and a mate George Smith. A couple of verses ran:

> *A wee Glasgow woman came pushin her pram*
> *Roarin and screaming up at a masked man.*
> *Hey Ronnie ya eedgit come doon when you can*
> *So's I can go hame to ma bed.*
>
> *But Ronnie was roarin back down to his wife*
> *Get hame to your mother and get on with your ain life,*
> *Big Slasher is up here and he's wieldin a big knife*
> *I wish I was back in my cell.*

Subsequent verses in this clever bit of songwriting referred to Sammy 'The Bear' Ralston and his troubles with the prison officers. Typical Glasgow humour and music making!

At one stage earlier in the day there had been hopes that the siege was about to end. Eight prisoners gave themselves up voluntarily. Any optimism around also got a boost when the prisoners appeared willing to give hostage Andrew Smith up in a deal involving Sammy Ralston. Andrew Smith had been led onto the roof to make a plea for his life and that of David Flanagan and John Kearney. He used a megaphone captured by the prisoners during the siege to say: 'Please don't send anyone in – our lives are going to be in danger.' He told reporters that the hostages were all 'fine'. The prisoners were aware that this was the day Sammy 'The Bear' Ralston was making an appearance in Glasgow Sheriff Court on an unconnected civil matter. And indeed he did appear in court with stitching and heavy bruising apparent to the public. The offer made by the prisoners was that they would free Officer Smith if they were allowed to see Ralston in B Block for themselves. The offer was given some consideration.

But the mood of the mob on the roof swung again when the periodic chants, songs and threats were silenced as the inmates listened on a small transistor radio to reports from the court that confirmed Ralston's appearance. The megaphone was back in action: 'The man was all bruised in court, dished out by the fascist brigade.' Ralston's family were similarly angry. His mother Agnes said: 'When the riot started I asked myself why are they doing this? Then I learned my son had been beaten up and stretchered out of B-Hall.' She claimed that other prisoners had seen him and that this is what started the protest. Agnes Ralston went on: 'It is hard to ask them to come down when you see the state of Sam's face. They are frightened to come off the roof in case it happens to them.'

These were comments from outside the prison walls. But wearing heavy prison clothing in the bitter cold and flaunting captured riot helmets, the protestors continued in the same vein. 'There is brutality throughout this prison. We demand an inquiry – a public inquiry, not an internal one, not a whitewash. We have human rights like everyone else. We are not exactly angels but that does not give them the right to treat us the way they do. We will only come out on stretchers.'

During the entire day negotiations were being conducted by specially trained prison officers working in shifts and shouting up at the rioters high above them on the roof. As in all such situations, rumours abound. At one stage the talks break down, at another they make progress. For anyone not directly involved it is difficult to really know what is going on. One development was that the hostages were seen to take hot drinks given to them. The prison authorities were trying to play tough but supplies of heating, lighting and water were maintained to B-Hall.

The next day brought some real hope for the first time that the siege might end. The 16 inmates barricaded in B-Hall agreed to release Andrew Smith, one of the three officers being held hostage. This was in return for a promise of food. Right at the start of the siege, on the Monday, the rooftop rioters claimed to have enough food for a month, but by the Wednesday they were hungry and the provision of food was a negotiating tool for the authorities. So Andrew Smith was given up in return for food for the other two hostages and the rioters. Mr Smith was reunited with his wife and examined by a medical man and told his colleagues that he had not been physically harmed. Earlier in the day soup and sandwiches had been sent in for hostages and their captors alike. But as the cold January hours passed, something a little more in the way of what Glaswegians would call a meal was required.

By nightfall after the release of Andrew Smith, the inmates and remaining hostages, David Flanagan and John Kearney, were seen tucking into large plates of the much favoured Glasgow culinary classic, pie, beans and chips. In another gesture, the rioters let the authorities pass letters from their wives to the hostages. The action and drama in the prison itself was now being shared with the involvement of the courts and politicians of all stripes.

As the macabre scene was played out on the rooftop of the great prison, the procurator fiscal's office and Strathclyde police were investigating accusations and counter accusations of assaults at the start of the siege. It was no surprise that Sammy Ralston, held in another of the prison's great halls, was involved. The cops said they were investigating an alleged assault on him and separately the fiscal's office issued a warrant for his arrest in connection with an assault on a prison officer.

The ban on visits was lifted that night to let Ralston's mother into the jail to see her son. She stayed for an hour, around teatime, and emerged to tell ITV's *News at Ten* that her son did not support the protest, though the perpetrators of the violence claimed to be demonstrating in his favour. 'They are only wasting their time,' she said. 'He doesn't like to see them up on the roof.' That Ralston was simply an excuse for the rioters seemed to be confirmed by reports that were now coming out of the prison on how the riots started. It was a trivial event that led to the most dramatic episode in the prison's long history. A row over some minor matter in the dining hall early on Monday morning had erupted into a full scale riot in a prison where, at the time, there was pent-up rage and anger, especially amongst the long-term prisoners.

After the siege was over, reports were to confirm that the mood in the prison had been ugly and dangerous for months, a mood fuelled by reports of unrest and riots in Saughton and Peterhead. There was no need for prisoners to have an ear to any grapevine to have their concerns heightened – the newspapers and television had been full of tales of trouble in the prison system for months.

It was reported during the riot that the start of it had been that incident in the dining hall. An officer trying to intervene had been hit over the head with a chair in true Wild West saloon fashion and other officers carried an inmate screaming and shouting away from the dining area. Mayhem broke out and other officers were hurt. The cause may have been trivial but the event was major.

After the end of the riot and the conclusion of the many trials and reports, newspapers were able to publish pictures of the devastation in B-Hall at the start and during the siege. The judge at the trial of some of the men involved called what was going on 'a torrent' of violence. The photographs graphically showed the damage – smashed cupboards, a floor littered with slates, lockers torn to bits, tea urns wrecked, furniture and crockery destroyed. The *Sunday Mail* had one remarkable picture of a hole in a wall of a cell. It had been dug out by trapped warders terrified that they were going to be burnt to death. Fearing berserk prisoners would set fire to mattresses placed against the cell doors, the officers frantically tried to escape, clawing at the walls with bare hands and makeshift tools. Their frantic efforts were accompanied by shouts from the cons of, 'We are going to get you, you bastards.' This led to a desperate, violent struggle between prisoners and guards and caused many of the injuries sustained by the officers. A total of 34 men were hurt, some seriously, others suffering minor injuries in what was virtually hand-to-hand fighting. Eventually they ran to safety through a hail of missiles thrown at them from above. Some did not make it. They became hostages.

The release of Andrew Smith was followed late on the Thursday with a second hostage, David Flanagan, being handed back to the authorities as a 'gesture of goodwill' and this was followed some hours later with the final hostage, John Kearney, being allowed to join his colleagues outside the beleaguered B-Hall. This happened after supplies of hot food and drink had been sent into the prison for the remaining rioters, now reduced to eleven, as four had left their redoubt earlier.

The riot was over, ending peacefully 'with a cuppa' as the papers said. After five days of drama and violence the end was remarkably low key with comforting words shared over a cup of tea with Father John McGinley. The prisoners had asked to see a chaplain. The authorities had agreed that the protesters would be examined medically, given access to their lawyers and visits from their families. But there was to be one final act of defiance – shortly after nine on the Friday morning, the last rump of the rioters clambered back on to the roof for the last time to sing 'We shall overcome' before returning to the wrecked hall to effectively surrender.

The wonder of it was that no one had died; no one was seriously hurt. No doubt chaplains, prison officers, some of the prisoners, and the public, who had been watching the drama play out for almost a week, thanked God for that.

2

BULLY BOYS, COLD CUSTARD
AND A POWDER KEG

The end of Scotland's longest siege of its kind (110 hours as opposed to 92 the previous year in Peterhead) posed the inevitable question: why did it happen? The public perception was largely that it was all down to the alleged brutality of warders dealing with difficult prisoners. It was a popular pub-talk theory. Everyone was airing his or her thoughts on the cause, especially folk who had never seen the inside of a prison other than on television. In the aftermath of an infamous episode in the history of the great prison everyone was suddenly an expert on penal matters.

In the days immediately after the surrender of the rioters, an 'insider' effectively knocked on the head the notion that it was all down to brutality by officers by saying that it was not as simple as a few rogue officers, the bad apples of the prison service, attacking some of the wild men in their charge. Tom Brown, one of the most respected commentators on current affairs in Scotland, then working for the *Record*, interviewed a man with another take on what caused the riot in Barlinnie and the previous, similar, disturbances in Peterhead and Saughton. The interviewee was described as an old lag, but it was said you could never tell that to look at him. This was an expert in the penal system, a man now successfully going straight who had done time in Scotland's toughest jails and also in Wandsworth and Albany in England. The *Record* called him 'Steve' and he minced no words: 'The riots were not caused by brutality from warders or the harsh regime. They were caused by men who live by violence in or out of prison.'

It was a well reasoned piece by a man with front line experience of the penal system. He must have surprised many who want prison regimes liberalised when he said: 'Of all the prisons I was in, those with the most liberal regime – where prisoners were not closely supervised and where you might not see an officer for hours – were by far the worst to serve time in.'

Most prisoners keep their head down when inside, some will console themselves with the old mantra of the lawbreaker, 'if you do the crime, you do the time'. When career criminals embarked on a life of villainy they knew the risks. Many old lags have told me that this is the most effective way to do your 'porridge', keep your nose clean and take advantage of every chance of education and entertainment you get when in the nick. Aim at the earliest possible release. Steve seemed to share this philosophy. According to him the jails with the easy going regimes were where what he called the bully boys ruled and the weakest of the prisoners go to the wall.

He also pointed out that prisons have areas set aside for inmates seeking 'protection' under Rule 43, which is designed to give safe haven to prisoners who feel threatened by their companions behind bars. Under Rule 43 he claimed he had never seen such a section empty. He added, 'It says something about life in jail that prisoners have to seek protection from their own kind. But I have never yet heard of a prisoner having to seek protection from the staff. I have seen and heard a lot of violent behaviour. Often I have seen prisoners assault other prisoners for no good reason. But I have never heard of staff making an UNPROVOKED attack on a prisoner.'

His view was that most prison officers are ordinary men doing a thankless job with the best of intentions. He said that in every case he had heard of, where prisoners and staff were in physical conflict, there was always a reason. He told of officers being drenched by the contents of a prisoner's chamber pot – 'and you can hardly blame them for being a bit tough with a guy who does that.'

Steve had also seen first hand how difficult it is for staff to restrain an inmate bent on mayhem, going 'bersie' as they say. People get hurt – on both sides of the dispute. A prison chaplain confirmed that to me with memories of seeing prison 'incidents' where, say half a dozen officers were trying to control a couple of guys running wild. In such a melee officers could hurt each other. These days officers are much better trained in restraint techniques, to the benefit of prisoner and officer.

Steve introduced what some might say was a racial element. He claimed that life was easier in English prisons because the inmates there had mostly committed crimes for profit while in Scotland many inmates were simply classic hard men who fought for the hell of it. Sometimes these hard men would coerce fellow inmates to join them in a violent struggle against authority. Especially if the hard man was in for years and had little to lose. Steve's verdict on the cause of the riot of '87 was simple. Blame the prison bully boys.

It was a pertinent point, but it shared the media attention with some rather complacent political views from people who ought to have known better. No one, not even the pub experts, believed that overcrowding in jails was the only reason for the tension and unrest. But it seems odd, at this distance in time, to suggest that overcrowding was not a contributory factor, especially since this was still in the era of the hideous practice of slopping out. John Renton, the respected long-time head of the Scottish Prison Officers Association, had told the media that overcrowding and undermanning were largely to blame for the riot. It was a view dismissed in a radio interview by Scottish Secretary Malcolm Rifkind who said he thought it unlikely that the spark that started the incident was overcrowding. Politicians of all stripes like a little spin, and Malcolm Rifkind pointed out on the airwaves that out of a Scottish prison population of around 5,000 or so, only around 50 were involved in trouble; the rest were behaving responsibly. But it has to be said that the 50 or so were doing a good job in grabbing headlines and wrecking jails. And terrifying their captors.

Another Tory to claim that Barlinnie was not overcrowded was Scottish Office Minster Ian Lang and he, too, was taken to task by John Renton who said, 'Overcrowding is a problem that will not go away and it is wrong of Mr Lang to say B-Hall is not overcrowded. The mixture of short and long term and remand inmates in Barlinnie is dangerous and can be damaging. Frankly if the inmates are trying to demonstrate they can take over prisons, they do not have to show us that. It is obvious that institutions cannot be run without the co-operation of prisoners.' Incidentally, the mix of convicted prisoners and untried men played a major role in a riot in Barlinnie in the thirties, a tale told later in this book. Another serious concern in the prison service was over the inadequacy of training for the country's 2,700 officers. It was said they were being denied 'in service' training because of pressure of work. Disturbingly Mr Renton said that the caring aspects of the job were being overshadowed by the custodial ones.

This argy-bargy and blaming began to obscure the fact that the crisis in the prisons had not just jumped up and grabbed the front pages. A Prison Inspectorate report on visits made to Barlinnie before the riot bore out John Renton's observations on training. It said that staff training was almost non-existent and staff facilities barely adequate though it did say the staff continued to carry out their duties conscientiously. But the danger to the morale of the officers was pointed out. This report was also highly critical of the number held on remand (35% of the prison population at that time) and the fact that these prisoners were held in conditions inferior to the convicted inmates. It stated categorically that there was overcrowding, little recreation and no opportunity of work for remand prisoners. The report also said that the overcrowding was restricted to doubling up, which was felt by many staff and governors to be preferable to trebling up, in cells designed in the 1880s to hold just one prisoner.

All the signs of a build-up of tension were in place. Little wonder then that when the lid finally blew off the pressure cooker, the cause was that trivial incident in a dining hall. Incidentally the inspectors were not impressed by that dining area and criticized the cleanliness of the place, tables not properly washed, dirt encrusted Formica and hot food being brought out too soon. It was said that soup and custard was seen stacked on hot plates up to two hours before meal time. The food serving system was primitive and 'hygiene was suspect'. Another problem that would contribute to the tension in the jail was the question of visiting. All visits were in closed conditions with a permanent transparent screen between visitor and prisoner. It was said that 'such arrangements have now been superseded in most prisons by open visiting and it is regrettable that no progress has yet been possible in Barlinnie owing to lack of facilities'. Another ingredient in the recipe for a prison powder keg.

Little wonder that the staff were as overwrought as the prisoners. This was a hellish place to work at that time. No surprise then that at one stage in the actual riot an angry prison officer confronted the press corps, who were covering the event with millions of pounds worth of technology, and screamed, 'This would never have happened if you had not been here. Why don't you all fuck off?' This loss of temper was perhaps justifiable in the circumstances – at the time the angry officer said it, three colleagues had knives at their throat. They could have died. But did his outburst have any validity? It was a concern that engaged the attention of *Herald* writer Allan Laing and there was no doubt there was a media circus on Barlinnie's doorstep (including the *Glasgow Herald* it must be said).

The logistics of covering such a riot are formidable. For example, the newspapers, radio and television had deployed hundreds of journalists to the site of the action. The television crews from down south, reporting back to the national networks, had 'scanner' trucks each worth around a million pounds. And some of the English hacks did not take full account of the fact that they were in the east end of Glasgow. One left a £25,000 camera in the back seat of his car covered with a jacket. It walked, no doubt something that some of the inmates across the road behind the walls would have found delightfully ironic. In the previous sieges at Peterhead and Saughton, intervention by tabloid journalists had helped break the deadlock. This time the Scottish Office and the prison authorities seemed determined to talk themselves out of this problem on their own. In the early days, the press circus was assembled just 100 yards outside the walls and the prisoners could play to the crowd asking the hacks to wave if they could hear them. And men shouting from the rooftops politely referred to the media pack as 'ladies and gentlemen'. But on the second full day of unrest the press and cameramen were moved back by the authorities further away from the walls, and the protestors, 'for their own safety'. It was not a comfortable story to cover. For some in the coldest week of a cold winter it was takeaway sandwiches and coffee as they waited shivering as events unfolded. ITN, up from London, aroused some envy with their big spending – they booked their entire entourage into an exclusive suite in a local pub. It was an exciting time for Glasgow newspaper people, and to this day when snappers and scribblers meet to reminisce over a pint or ten, old memories flood back and tales, both serious and amusing, are told.

Glasgow photographer Alastair Devine, much lauded internationally for his studies of celebrities (everyone from Gordon Ramsey to Jane Russell) was in his twenties and working for the *Daily Record* at the time. He remembers it well. The fiery tabloid, even then, was the ideal place for a photographer to learn the wrinkles of the trade from the hard life and hard graft on the streets of this tough city. When news of the rooftop riot broke he was phoned at home and told by Martin Gilfeather of the *Record* picture desk to pitch up at Barlinnie at six a.m.. It was completely dark when he arrived and there were just one or two other frozen photographers there, colleagues from the Glasgow press and a few curious Glasgow punters wondering what was going on. Alastair Devine remembers one such who enquired, 'Hey, big man, any chance of a look through your camera?' Alastair, always sympathetic to the punter, ignored the irony of the appellation 'big man', a typical Glasgow form of address, being used about him, as he drew himself up to his full five feet eight inches and stood back while the guy took a squint through the telephoto lens at the roof and the masked and caped figures there. He was impressed. 'Fucking magic,' he remarked as he stepped back from the tripod. Even the cops on occasion asked for a look through the powerful telescopic lenses to see if they could recognise any rioters. One raised a laugh with his colleagues when he spotted someone he had nicked in the past remarking: 'Aye it's him right enough, Clint Easterhouse'. Another cop recognised a prisoner nick-named 'The Pigeon' after the amount of time he had spent on rooftops.

Available light is always a real concern for any news photog-rapher. The light during the siege was, of course, winterish and poor as you would expect in Glasgow in a grim January and only lasted from around nine until four. Alastair remembers it as giving a curious grainy 'middle east' feel to the pictures, though some of the best photos were taken on the odd dry cold day with clear blue skies. In particular the minutes around sunrise as the light slowly wrapped itself around the tall chim-neys and the grey stone of the jail and the bizarre shapes of the rioters were silhouetted on the roof were productive for photographers of an arty state of mind. The snappers were largely dressed in woolly hats, warm duffel coats or full news-paper issue foul weather gear with layer upon layer of sweaters and knitwear, necessary since most of the time they were standing still watching the rooftop protesters for any move-ment that would make a picture. Unlike the cosseted ITN hacks, coffee in plastic cups, curled sandwiches and greasy mutton pies were the order of the day.

Alastair Devine makes a wry observation that the prison full of hard men had on its roof the hardest of the hard. How they survived long hours up there in the winter winds, rain and chill is a testimony to their anger at what was going on in the prison and their street-hard Glasgow toughness. Alastair Devine remembers the reporters and photographers covering the riot postulating that the current protest was part of some sort of organised unrest in Scottish jails suggesting that the demos at Saughton and Peterhead were part of the same plot. There was, however, no real link between the three riots. The photographers were also of the opinion that the Barlinnie hard men might have done better to wait for warmer weather before taking to the roof.

The five-day vigil of the photographers was not without laughs. One hack turned up with a football one day and with the cameras still trained on the roof the snappers had a quick game of five-a-side. The long hours of waiting and watching gave life to a lot of banter and joke telling.

The rioters knew full well how the pictures and the publicity were helping their cause and publicising the alleged brutality they were demonstrating against. This was helpful to the photographers. When one prisoner posed precariously on top of a high chimney pot hundreds of feet up and raised his hands wide in a crucifixion gesture, the photographers realised the significance, though the move had slightly taken them by surprise. Several of the camera men immediately stood up mimicking the arms apart gesture and the prisoner took the hint, repeated his 'crucifixion' pose and a great picture went into the papers and photo archives.

However over the top the media attention was at times, the question of whether or not it contributed to the troubles at the prison is easily answered. As Allan Laing said in a perceptive piece: 'Perhaps we should leave the prison service, the police – and why not the Government – to deal with everything and our performing circus will turn a blind eye. Do that and we destroy accountability and eventually freedom of speech and democracy. Maybe then in 20 years or so we would all be standing on prison rooftops in protest. And the circus would have disappeared for ever.'

All this was when the papers were still hot off the press, as it were, and tempers still high. And the various court cases that were a product of the riot were still to happen. In the end nine men stood trial for their part in the riot and three – Allan McLeish, William Marshall and Hugh Twigg – were found guilty and sentenced to a total of 22 years. Sammy Ralston also had a sentence increased. So it is interesting to read of the official reaction which came in a report on the prison in 1990. The actual riot and hostage taking was covered in the previously mentioned brief official factual description of what had happened. But nonetheless the full report was peppered with criticisms, some echoing negative comments made down the years in official reports and others that had been raised in Parliament before the practice of regular reporting on individual prisons had been started.

This 1990 report was 'far from impressed' by the accommodation provided and in the conditions in which many inmates lived. D-Hall came in for some serious criticism. It had reopened in 1989 after renovation but at the time of the inspection only half the hall was in use, the top two floors waiting for their turn for renovation. 'Conditions in the occupied flats was marginally better than in the other halls but the excessive use of posters and the lack of chamber pots were again most evident. Cell furniture, too, was not in good repair. Poor ventilation and the problem of cell windows fixed shut also obtained here.' It went on to say that on the top floor the lack of maintenance was evident and that the cells were dirty and not wind or water tight and broken windows gave access to birds to roost in the cells, adding to the unsightly mess.

These reports were couched in classic civil service language, but the meaning is clear and unambiguous. For example the description of accommodation in Barlinnie at that time was 'disappointingly depressing'. Some cell furniture was described as 'decrepit' and 'unacceptable'. The toilet facilities were also criticised: 'The shortage of chamber pots in use is a matter of some concern. Barlinnie is an old prison with no integral or night sanitation facilities. It is a matter of propriety therefore that chamber pots, with properly fitting lids, be available in each cell. In many cells we found no such provision, or plastic gallon containers which are not designed for such usage. The lack of a proper in-cell container for sanitary purposes merely encourages inmates, after evening lock up, to resort to unacceptable and unsanitary practice.' It does not take much to imagine what really went on – and this is a report on conditions in the biggest prison in Scotland in the late eighties, not at the start of the twentieth century or earlier. It is perhaps somewhat comforting to note that those charged with overseeing how our prisoners are treated approach the matter with some humanity – though their language is unemotional. What is not comforting is to read one report after another and the dispiriting comments that areas of criticism mentioned earlier have not been properly addressed. Everyone in the prison service knows that to be deprived of your liberty is a huge punishment and that it is wrong to 'animalise' or 'monsterise' criminals in the way that such controversial figures as Jimmy Boyle claim happened to them in the days before the Special Unit was formed. But the very fabric of places like Barlinnie in those days must have contributed much to the unrest and the dangers to the staff.

The 1990 report, which covered the period from June 1986, six months before the riot, until 1990, shows that the warning signs of trouble were all there, even if some officers did not see them, and it also pinpointed problems even after the famous surrender of the hostage takers. For example it stated that without doubt that Barlinnie was becoming more and more unsatisfactory in terms of amenity for both staff and inmates – discipline and control began to diminish and disciplinary offences by inmates increased significantly. It painted a picture of a prison on the verge of being out of control. During the period from July 1986 to the beginning of January (when the hostage taking began) fires were started in cells on nine occasions and at other locations twice. There were also several attempts at fire-raising which only the vigilance of the staff prevented from causing serious damage or perhaps danger to life. Most of the cell fires took place in the remand hall and these were accompanied by many other acts of indiscipline and defiance.

The report went on to make the totally understandable comment that after an incident like the siege itself it might have been imagined that there would be a lessening of incidents and a return to something approaching normality. Not so. In fact it was reported that indiscipline and confrontation continued to an even greater degree. Eventually in October '87 the prison was considered out of control and a 'lock down' took place to facilitate a new start. The road back to relative health for the establishment that is HMP Barlinnie was long and tortuous. But gradually the Governor Andrew Gallagher, and his successor Alan Walker, succeeded in bringing the place back under control. A visit in the dark days in the aftermath by Princess Anne was helpful. She spoke freely to a number of prisoners and Governor Alan Walker said that the visit meant a lot to the prison, staff and inmates alike.

In the days immediately after the siege staff morale had plummeted; indeed at one stage industrial action was imminent. But a combination of factors turned the place around. Some improvement to the overcrowding took place, the number of officers on sick leave was reduced, staffing was increased and greater discipline imposed. As it moved into the last decade of the twentieth century the prison was becoming at least a slightly better place for prisoners and staff. But there were more dramas to come.

3

WAITING FOR A CO-PILOT
AND OTHER MISERIES

The story of how Barlinnie came to be built has an unsettling denouement. In the 1880s those in charge of the prison service in and around Glasgow concluded that due to overcrowding in the existing jails a new, and massive, prison was needed. The original plan called for a gigantic four-block structure with each block holding 200 prisoners. It was visionary thinking at a time when the public largely could not care less about the inmates of the jails. 'Let them rot' was the popular thinking at that time. So it is greatly to the credit of reformers that the plan for a new building went through.

However, on completion, the number of prisoners almost immediately exceeded expectations and a fifth block had to be added. It is truly sad to have to acknowledge in 2011 that at no time in its almost 130 years of existence has Barlinnie consistently held the numbers it was designed to cope with. What chance has rehabilitation really had in all those years? Any dreams the early prison reformers had of Barlinnie as a place where wrongdoers could be steered back on the path of a productive and legal life in society were blighted, made much more difficult if not impossible by overcrowding. The fact is that the prison has been overcrowded by a factor of at least 50 per cent year after year. The dream of the 1880s of five halls and 1,018 prisoners has virtually never been achieved. A fact that is as astonishing as it is depressing.

The ex-Governor, Bill McKinlay, is on record on more than one occasion saying that the place should be knocked down and rebuilt: 'Overcrowding is not acceptable when we have two people to a cell that was built in the nineteenth century for one person.' No rational person could disagree with that. Especially anyone who has visited the jail and seen the physical dimensions of the cells. It is chilling to imagine years spent in such physical confinement, never mind the complete removal of your freedom. But even in such cells humour can spring from a dark corner. Speaking to one young lad with almost a year still to go to freedom but enjoying – if that is the word – a few weeks in a cell to himself, he remarked that this privilege would soon end and that he expected a 'co-pilot' any day soon, this being current prison slang for cell sharing.

One of the problems of cell sharing is choosing partners for each prisoner. Those whose experience of prison life has been garnered from sitting in an armchair with a coffee to hand watching Ronnie Barker as 'habitual criminal' Norman Stanley Fletcher in TV's *Porridge* and laughing at the banter between him and his young cellmate, Godber, played by Richard Beckinsale have a rose-tinted view. It really isn't like that. Nearer the truth is the old joke of the accountant finding himself sharing a cell with an old lag. He tells his new acquaintance that he is in for fraud and asks the villain what he is inside for. His companion tells him he's also in for 'white collar' crime – he strangled a minister.

The problem is however no joke. Though as many a prison officer will tell you humour is vital in such a place and the staff are conscious of the difference between laughing with the inmates and laughing at them. The issue of who shares a cell receives serious and in-depth risk assessment. But it is a certainty that however well intentioned and thorough such an assessment is there will be occasional errors, adding to the misery of inmates.

An eloquent comment on cell sharing – underlining its problems – was made in a letter in 2001 to the then Governor Roger Houchin by Brian Quail, a protestor against nuclear weapons who was sentenced to a week in jail for refusing to pay a £30 fine. It was a lengthy and critical piece of prose looking at prison life from the viewpoint of a non-smoking 63-year-old who had a double coronary bypass – and no previous experience of prisons. He wrote: 'In general I found the most repellant aspect to my imprisonment to be the total lack of privacy. To be compelled to spend 23 hours a day in close confinement with another person, sharing every bodily function with them, was unpleasant in the extreme.'

He went on: 'More than anything I yearned to be alone. Solitary confinement seemed my idea of bliss. In such solitude, prison would offer me a valuable opportunity for study, meditation and prayer. I must repeat imprisonment should mean the loss of freedom, not loss of privacy. That is an additional and unwarranted affliction.'

Brian Quail also pointed out that his chest problems made him ask for a no-smoking cell, but he was told that was impossible. He says in his letter: 'I consequently spent 23 hours a day with a cellmate who smoked constantly, even waking up several times during the night to do so. I feel that this was an assault on my health.'

This is just one example of how unacceptable overcrowding can be. It was one lone voice, but thousands must have thought those very thoughts even if they did not have the literary skills to write a letter to the 'Gov'. Overcrowding was as unacceptable in 1882 as it is in 2011. Indeed, it is almost incomprehensible that a supposedly enlightened society can accept the existence of such a place as the Bar-L. Even more incomprehensible is that slopping out – another item dealt with in the Quail letter – was tolerated until a few years ago, but that is another story told in detail later in this book.

At one time there were eight prisons in Glasgow, an unsurprising indication that the place was no stranger to lawlessness in years past as it is today, but by 1840 only two remained. One was the North Prison at Duke Street, known as the 'Bridgewall', which closed in 1955, and the other the South Prison at Glasgow Green known as the 'Burgh'. On the decision to build a new prison to alleviate overcrowding in these two establishments, the Barlinnie Farm Estate was approached about the purchase of thirty-two-and-a-half acres of land on which the prison now stands. The farm sold the land for the sum of £9,750 and building began. Great thought had gone into the choice of site and the area chosen had many advantages; indeed it seemed ideal for the purpose.

It was out in the country, far from the teeming tenements that would provide such a ready supply of inmates. This also meant that it was not overlooked by housing as it is now. Old mining sites were often a problem in the east end of Glasgow, but the chosen area promised no problems from this difficulty either. The ground lay on a bed of whinstone, there were quarries (handy for backbreaking hard labour) and it was free of dampness. And it lay adjacent to the Monklands canal where a wharf could be built to facilitate delivery of supplies of all kinds, including building materials.

Inside its high walls Barlinnie has something of the feel of a miniature town. Though, not surprisingly, a town without much joy in its heart. These days the outside walls of some of the halls are adorned with little flower baskets, but even in summer the blooms in these little 'nods in the direction of suburbia' look strangely unhealthy, as if they, too, long for freedom outside the walls. Even walking around in the rain it feels like 'prison rain', not the wind-borne free sheets of water that frequently drop on you when outside the walls. There is an atmosphere of confinement in this place that seeps into anyone and anything inside it.

Just beyond the reception, in an open area, stands a huge bell on a frame. This is believed to be from the original farm in the area and was used to signal the start and finish of work. It hangs silently, again as if stilled by the atmosphere of confinement around it.

The original farm manager's office and home was built around by the architect and is now part of the prison Health Centre. A-Hall was commissioned in July 1882 when it officially became a 'place of legal detention' and the first three prisoners arrived on 15 August that year. This was big news in the city and the old *Evening Citizen* reported it in depth even if the tone was less sensational than that required of current tabloid reporters:

'The new jail in course of construction at Barlinnie has now been so far completed as to admit it being opened today. There was no formal ceremony to mark its inauguration, Her Majesty's Commissioners merely legislating the building as one of the Scotch *(sic)* prisons from this date. As every visitor to the eastern extremity of the city is aware, the new edifice stands on a green acclivity a short distance from Cumbernauld Road and about 100 yards to the south of the Monklands Canal, near Gartcraig. It is built of light coloured sandstone and surrounded by a high white boundary wall, has a massive imposing aspect and can be seen from all directions for a considerable distance.

'It was the original intention of the Commissioners to construct four erections – each formed in a single block – and the whole structure to contain 800 cells. Whether this will be carried out is not yet definitely known though there is no reason to conclude that there will be any departure from the plans as first advanced. Meanwhile Block A has been finished and looks a very substantial and secure piece of workmanship. It is four storeys high with 50 cells in each storey thus making a total of 200 cells. The second block 'B' – each section being constructed of the same height and style – is expected to be ready later in the summer.

'A house has been erected for the Governor to the south of the prison and he and a staff of officers have already entered their new quarters. The prisoners have not yet taken up their abode in Barlinnie but some will be sent this week. It is not yet stated how Duke Street Jail is to be disposed of – whether it will be kept as a jail or eventually given up. It will at least be required for a considerable time yet.'

The *Citizen* man certainly got this right since Duke Street was open for another 70 years or so!

All prisons get regular inspections and Barlinnie, and in particular some of its governors, have on occasion fallen foul of the inspectors who down the years did not pull their punches when they found something not meeting with their approval. And, of course, in these days of instant communication their findings get a good airing in the press and on TV. But the Bar-L got off to a good start with the Inspectorate and the first report on the new prison, covering 1882–3, was pretty upbeat. It said that the prisoners were kept industriously and constantly employed and that the prisoners were generally well behaved.

And any instances of severe punishment for misbehavior were 'exceptions'. The surgeon was also reported to have been constant and attentive to his duties. The general health of the prison was quoted as 'good'. The food was also inspected and found to be 'of good quality'.

However the first Governor, a former navy man, Captain Montieth, became seriously ill after just four months in charge and had to be replaced with a Mr J Taylor, a former governor of Ayr prison. He ran the show until Major W Dodd took over in April 1883. Incidentally, to date there have been 22 governors though Mr Taylor who returned as top man in 1888, and stayed in the post for ten years, is the only officer to have held the number-one job twice. The short reference to prisoners being kept employed didn't really tell the full story – the list of what went on in the workshops is impressive: baking, basket weaving, blacksmithing, tinsmithing, plumbing, carpet beating, carpentry, firewood chopping, mat making, oakum teasing, ships fender making, shoe making and repairing, weaving, and mattress making were just some of the tasks carried out in the work sheds.

Outside there was the labour in the quarry. An early concession to health and safety saw the quarry work parties issued with gauze to make primitive goggles to protect the eyes as hammers swung in rhythm breaking up the local stone and converting it into aggregate for use in the building of B, C, and D halls, which were completed between 1883 and 1892. It was already becoming clear that more cells were needed and in 1892/93 the perimeter wall was extended and by 1897 the fifth hall, E-Hall, was completed. It is still possible to see where the original stone of the perimeter wall changes to roughcast concrete in the extension. This took the capacity up to around 900 prisoners, a figure often doubled in modern times. In the first year or so of the life of the prison, the full staff complement was a governor and a deputy, a chaplain, a medical officer, a steward, six clerks, a matron, two male teachers and two female teachers, 43 male warders, 19 female warders, and three 'other officers', two male, one female. An early part of the huge building project that was Barlinnie was the completion in 1889 of 39 'married warders' quarters' outside of the prison.

Proof that the forward thinking of people involved in prison reform was not completely swept away by the concern of over-crowding is shown by the fact that, as early as 1890, a gymnasium was built. And at the centre of the prison, surrounded by the massive halls is the church – completed in 1893 – an impressive demonstration of how seriously the Victorians took religious matters. Even today, when it is used for drama productions by groups like Theatre Nemo, a charity theatre company with a mission to promote good mental health and wellbeing through the creative arts – such as animation, taiko drumming and drama – it is a striking place to visit. Incidentally Theatre Nemo have been facilitating workshops in various Scottish prisons and have a strong relationship with Barlinnie which has been built up over the past seven years.

It is interesting that at this time there is a huge movement to promote community drumming whether it be samba or taiko or fife and drum (the origin of the country blues and bread and butter to the Scottish regiments!)

There are good reasons for this:

Drumming is good physical exercise.

Drumming is catharctic – it is a kind of 'beating' after all – and it may be emotionally healthy.

Drumming involves counting, listening, and rhythm; it is therefore good brain exercise.

Drumming is often thought to have a spiritual element due to its capacity to induce trance-like states.

Drumming is seen by some as having a 'natural' element – establishing contact with ancient folk memory and as such making contact with nature and primitive man (fanciful but not impossible).

Drumming promotes dancing and singing which also have social/community and health-giving qualities.

Perhaps most importantly, drumming promotes community and closeness – historically drums have always been played where people gather, encouraging togetherness and uniformity (think of the Scottish military marching band versus African tribal dancing).

A single drum is a rather sad thing . . . lots of drums are dramatic.

On a more subtle angle, the men's movement wanted to reclaim drumming – it is a peculiarly male and even warlike activity and as such it may be appropriate in all-male settings such as prisons where a macho culture might link some 'artistic' and creative enterprises with femininity and the effete.

Drum beats affect things like pulse, breathing rate, the speed you drive at etc, and many people firmly believe that drumming and similar rhythmic activity (any music/poetry) helps us modify our emotions and moods. Exercise is regularly prescribed for people with depression; drumming and music therapy are often also recommended.

Because drumming can be threatening (due to its warlike component) and often involves strong emotional release, it is not suitable for a compulsory curriculum . . . but if people have the opportunity to opt in, they mostly do! It is a good move to use it in prison theatre.

Sitting in the Kirk in Barlinnie for a normal service or maybe some quiet contemplation, it's possible for a brief period to forget you are in a penal institution. It is perhaps the only place in the whole of the establishment where it is possible to feel 'outside' inside, because it is so like a normal place of worship.

A prison of this size is constantly evolving and almost every year there has been change. In 1967 there was a major extension to the perimeter to create the present industrial complex where the production of shelving and garden furniture has taken over from oakum teasing and the like. In the new work sheds the prisoners learn, under the watchful gaze of trained instructors, the techniques of state of the art timber cutting and fabrication. This is a costly service to provide and because of the prison environment the equipment cannot be used in a fully commercial way and the hours of operation are necessarily restricted. Whatever the prisoners make is sold, but it does little to contribute financially to the millions a year it takes to run the prison. Which is a pity, but the operation in the work sheds, particularly working with timber, is a valuable introduction to normal life for many of the prisoners who have no experience of a factory environment. Or indeed of regular work. The creation of valuable artifacts is also, for many, a much-needed source of satisfaction in such a grim place. One snag is that because of the continual rotation of prisoners from one establishment to another, and some of the shorter sentences being served, it is not possible at the moment for prisoners to get work qualifications that would help them to jobs on the outside.

The years since the *Evening Citizen* reported on the light-coloured sandstone walls dominating the east end of the city have seen that stone turn grimy, blackened by the smoke of factories and coal fires from the houses that soon sprang up round the walls. A bit of sandblasting would not go amiss though there are other more pressing priorities – like the almost constant refurbishing of the internal facilities. This does not come cheap. The refurbishment of D-Hall for example, completed in 1997, cost £5 million.

Other milestones in the life of the fabric of the prison included the surprising inclusion of fitting out a female section, needed because of the closure of Duke Street Prison in 1955 which had become the city prison for women. The cells used to hold the women sent to the Bar-L eventually became home to the Barlinnie Special Unit from 1972 to 1994, after female offenders were placed elsewhere.

These days the majority of women offenders in the west of Scotland are held at Cornton Vale near Stirling, a much more rural environment than that of Barlinnie. Around 230 women (including young offenders) are held there and it is interesting that a prison built as recently as 1975 is still having overcrowding problems and refurbishment programmes. No matter how thorough the long-term planning is, forecasts always seemed to be defeated by growing numbers of prisoners, of both sexes.

Despite the upgrading over the years there is no doubt that Barlinnie is showing its age, apart from the problems of overcrowding. Much money could still be spent profitably on improving conditions without going over the line that allows the tabloid pundits to rant on about it being a 'home from home' and a 'cushy lifestyle'. The library is a case in point. This is a key facility that should be heavily used. Sadly a considerable portion of the inmates have reading and educational problems that keep them out of the literary loop. But those who use the library would, in my opinion, benefit from a better browsing area and a few soft seats creating just a little of the ambience of a Waterstone's or the late, much-missed Borders (needless to say without the lattes and hot chocolate, never mind the muffins and croissants!). That would make it a better place to instill the reading habit.

Away from the library, close to the reception area, there exists a now unused, but undestroyed, area that would pop the eyes of anyone who believed life in prison was a cushy option: the dog boxes. These are mini windowless stone cells hardly the size of a cupboard. Now disused and discarded and, like shackles and the infamous Peterhead cages, redundant in the modern prison regime, they are one of the first things a prisoner sees. Their function was to hold prisoners in the queue for admission, waiting for their prison garb or waiting to move from one section to another. Here men were kept sitting in uncomfortable, constricting darkness. It was almost impossible to turn round and completely impossible to really stretch out. Inside a dog box you really knew you were 'inside'. And at least we have moved on from that. Some criminals I have interviewed down the years told me the dog boxes were the feature of life inside they hated most.

Among the most important areas of the prison – at least to the inmates – is the agents' room, where prisoners are allowed to confer with their lawyers. Down the years this too has been upgraded. Prison officers and the Governors have no trouble with inmates meeting their legal eagle of choice inside the prison walls. The prison service and the lawyers each appreciate they have a job to do, albeit different, and generally show each other mutual respect. In the Bar-L such famous pleaders as Laurence Dowdall, Joe Beltrami and Donald Findlay have listened to hard luck story after hard luck story from headline making murderers to fraudsters and burglars, even the small time crooks the prisoners themselves call 'gas meter bandits'. These are world-weary men who have heard it all before. But you can always get a surprise, even in Barlinnie. Frazer McCready, a lawyer now working in the Stirling area, with extensive criminal law experience, told me of a scary happening that also had its funny side. He was a raw, eager young lawyer visiting a couple of clients in the old agents' room. Unknown to Frazer, these two had had a bit of a falling out over a girl, a not unusual occurrence among the Glasgow criminal fraternity. When Frazer had finished chatting to the first guy, and getting his story down on to his legal note pad, the accused was taken away to a secure area to wait until the second interview was over, as he was under protection in the jail at the time.

Frazer says: 'I was halfway through seeing my second visit when the first accused who was being escorted back to his hall burst into the room, attacking my second client. They were both big guys and were soon knocking lumps out of each other. Extra officers were quickly on the scene following the alarm but they took a good five minutes to split them up. It was only after they were both taken away that one of the officers stated: "Was there no a lawyer in here? Oh fuck, where is he?" It was only then that they found me in an empty room across the hallway having done the only brave thing I could have thought of – crawled out on the floor during the barney. Fortunately neither of the love rivals was prosecuted – to my relief – as no doubt I would not have been in a position to act.'

One of Frazer's colleagues also had a humorous introduction to legal work in the Bar-L. In his case his client asked, at the start of the meeting, if he could stand on the legal eagle's chair. Frazer's pal did not want to upset the client and so got off his chair to allow the prisoner to climb on. He stood there for a few minutes staring through the bars and, when asked what he was doing, the prisoner replied he just wanted to look out the window – as he had not seen the outside world for the last two weeks!

*   *   *

The young Mr McCready's first impressions of Barlinnie, fresh from academia, was like that of most young lawyers. It was a big, cold, unfriendly place, but 'once you get over the initial shock of being in the jail it was not a bad place to visit. I would say most accused appreciate a visit from their lawyer – it breaks up the boredom of the place. Some accused simply ask you to stay on as long as possible and many's the time I've heard a prisoner saying, "could you not just stay a bit longer and talk to me?" '

One of the biggest changes Frazer McCready has noticed in recent years is the increase in prisoners with ethnic backgrounds in Barlinnie. Every visit with a non-English-speaking prisoner requires the assistance of a qualified translator. Given that most, if not all, remand prisoners are on legal aid, the State must be paying a fortune for translators. But, without doubt, it's all a necessary part of a fair system of justice. Incidentally that prison humour thing surfaced again on Frazer's first visit to a client in jail when a smiling warder suggested that a striped shirt was not a good idea if he wanted to get back out!

Not all visits by lawyers to the prison were jokey affairs. In 2006 a 32-year-old woman solicitor was jailed for supplying heroin and diazepam to an inmate, using the lawyers' consulting room as the place for the handover. Her defence was largely based on being coerced by a gangland figure into taking the drugs inside. The errant lawyer also had mental health concerns but, sentencing her in the High Court in Edinburgh, Lord Kinclaven said: 'Your case, like many others in this court, clearly illustrates the damage and the devastation that can be caused by involvement with drugs and the drugs trade. I have taken into account what has been said about the circumstances of the offending, coercion, pressure, threats of violence, reference to a handgun, fears for safety, the apparent lack of financial gain, the cooperation with the Crown, and the fact that your legal career is over. But I am satisfied that the court does require to impose a custodial sentence.'

As background to this interesting little tale of drugs and jail it should be pointed out that every day in life around 25% of the prison population of Barlinnie is dished out methadone from the in-house medical centre and that dealing with addictions is a major part of the reception process. Everyone in the jail is aware of the presence of illegal substances and the pressure on visitors to supply them and in this case the investigation began with a tip-off from an inmate.

So what is to be done with Barlinnie? Politicians of all stripes, one of the most respected Chief Prison Inspectors Dr Andrew McLellan, the ex-Governor McKinlay, and the Justice Secretary Kenny MacAskill were all on board the same train when interviewed by *Evening Times* man Russell Leadbetter recently. Dr McLellan warned that it was not just Barlinnie that was a problem – he said our entire prison system was facing crisis. A new jail or two would not solve the problem. Many are needed. Mr MacAskill praised the staff for doing an excellent job in difficult conditions with difficult people. In particular he said prison governors and staff in Scotland were 'manfully seeking to cope, but we have to lighten the load.'

Clearly one way to do that is to keep people who really should not be there out of prison, making more use of home detention curfews, community service and electronic tagging. Mr MacAskill will find few to disagree with his observation: 'If we are to allow them (prison staff) to do their proper job – to make sure people are punished but rehabilitated, and dangerous and serious criminals are incarcerated – we cannot continue to have prisons simply as a receptacle for people with minor problems committing minor offences.' That is blue sky thinking, but in itself will not solve the problem. More bricks and mortar are still required.

Back in the 1880s those in charge of the prison service were far-sighted enough to let the prisoners of Barlinnie help with the building of the new prison through their work in the prison quarry which provided building materials. Would it be an impractical fantasy if, in these enlightened days, we devised a plan to move prisoners from the Bar-L to new fit-for-purpose establishments little by little? Letting the prisoners assist in turning the five great halls of Barlinnie – A, B, C, D, and E – into dust would be the ultimate act of symbolism in society's attitude to the wrongdoer.

4

HUMAN RATS, CHESS AND OUT THROUGH THE WINDOW

The reputation of Barlinnie is a fearsome one to folk who live life on the right side of the law. As they glimpse it driving past on the M8 heading for the genteel delights of Edinburgh, ready for a credit card raid on the upmarket shops of the capital or a bite to eat and a moment or two of Mozart, a shiver can run down the spine. If they think about it at all in any depth, their imagination confers on the prison the status of the ultimate hell of life in Glasgow. The solid citizen may know little of what it is really like inside, but they know enough to make the thought of life behind bars in such a place the stuff of nightmares.

In this sense prison is truly a deterrent though it has to be pointed out that those who fear incarceration most are, in any case, those least likely to have their collar felt by a cop and taken on a trip to court, a lecture from a Sheriff or judge, and onward to 'the big hoose in the east end' in the famous blue bus (now replaced by vehicles provided by a private security company) shuttling between the prison and the courts. For anyone who has never been inside, it is revealing to hear the tales of old lags. The perception of the career criminal on jail life is, not surprisingly, rather different to that of the innocent.

Walter Norval is a case in point. The city's first Godfather was almost hungry to get into the place. A wild and lawless life in Maryhill which started with robbing wee sweetie shops and escalated to armed bank robbery and attempted murder had conditioned him for his first experience of Barlinnie. His youthful experiences with his gang known as 'the Wee Mob' had made it a certainty that long spells behind bars were sure to follow. And they did, starting in 1945 when he had been arrested after a robbery at a tobacconist's shop and found himself taken from Glasgow's Northern Police office to Barlinnie. Norval in his early days in Maryhill had rubbed against a couple of archetypical Glasgow hard men John Foy and Joe O'Hara, a duo who strutted around brawling and fighting at any opportunity. Collectively know as the 'Kings of the Garscube Road', they ran big money pitch and toss schools on the banks of the Forth and Clyde Canal among other nefarious ploys. They took a shine to young Walter who no doubt reminded them of the cocky fighting 'fuck 'em all' attitude of their own youth and their disrespect for the law. Walter spent hours listening to the tales of his criminal mentors. Tales that included experiences in Borstal, Barlinnie and other criminal establishments.

So it is not surprising that he had fixed in the back of his mind that doing time added street cred to the would-be hard man and gang leader. Many others in the criminal fraternity shared the belief that doing time in the Bar-L was a necessary step on the road to the top in crime. In a long career of lawbreaking, Norval would end up as something of an expert in penal establishments. A brief spell in the army as a conscript (he was pretty swiftly given an ignominious discharge, of course) saw him doing the rounds of some of the toughest jails in England. In the days of conscription in the forties and fifties, many a bolshie youth simply decided not to register and got away with it. Norval however was 'on the books' already, as it were, when he reached National Service age. His Borstal time saw to that. Fresh out of the infamous Polmont institution and back on the streets of Glasgow, hungry for trouble, he had to watch his back more carefully than most – the boys in blue were after him and so were the military police. As a fledgling hard man he was in no mood to volunteer to serve king and country.

But he was nabbed one night and found himself in Maryhill Barracks en route to Richmond in Yorkshire in the worst piece of recruitment the Green Howards ever made. He almost immediately did a runner back to Glasgow but was recaptured in a month or so. Back in uniform the series of inevitable courts martial began. After the first he was sent to Colchester military prison. Even at this stage he had, of course, sampled both Barlinnie (as an untried prisoner) and Borstal, but Colchester was something else. A natural-born member of the awkward squad, he spent long hours in what was called 'the wet cell', a stinking place reserved for hard cases.

This was a primitive place and prisoners were graded according to behaviour with privileges granted to those who conformed best. This created a sort of inverse league table of malcontents. True to character, Walter Norval was granted Stage One status – the lowest of the low or maybe you might just say the most difficult of the difficult. It was so bad that he had to get the help of a Status Three prisoner to get in on the 'snout' racket in the prison. Tobacco, its consumption and control, is a major player in any prison trouble. That was shown clearly in the Barlinnie riots in the 1930s (discussed later in this book) and it continues to this day in every prison in the land. Though now the problem is compounded by illegal drugs.

'Mad Scotsman' Norval was a serial deserter and was soon

back in Scotland, ending up on one occasion back in the Bar-L. There were dramatic scenes at the main gate at Barlinnie when his sentence ended and the military lay in wait for his exit. The army knew Walter Norval would not step quietly back into their arms so a jeep, with a corporal and three soldiers armed with rifles, was sent to collect him. Pushed out into the real world through the fearsome gates of the prison, he immediately threw himself on the ground and announced to the assembled military personnel, the prison officers and any of the good folk of Riddrie who happened to be around: 'I'm no' going'. The prison officers were convulsed with laughter at this bizarre street scene. The army swiftly started their manoeuvres, the military police unfazed by this somewhat ludicrous confrontation, and Norval was dragged at gunpoint into the jeep and driven to Central Station.

There the pantomime continued and the reluctant soldier had to be dragged onto a handy mail cart and wheeled the length of Platform One to the train for the south. It was a sight the douce Glasgow commuters who witnessed it are unlikely to forget. Back in the army, before his final discharge, Norval did the rounds of many infamous prisons including Shepton Mallet which, like Barlinnie, was once a place of execution. As in many such places there was talk of haunting by the criminals put to death.

One of the weapons that those in jail who protest their innocence use is the threat of hunger strikes. Barlinnie has had its share. When writing the life of Walter Norval, I spent months with him discussing his prison experience – which included years in Peterhead as well as incarceration in Barlinnie and spells in less arduous surroundings such as Dungavel and Penninghame. One morning as he supped his porridge – he had developed a lifelong taste for the prisoner's traditional breakfast – we talked, ironically in the circumstances, of hunger strikers. In one of the many military jails he spent time he gave it a try himself. According to him it is not as dramatic as it seems.

Apparently the torment of not eating is gradually replaced by a strange kind of mental state in which the desire to eat has been replaced with the overriding, even stronger, desire to prove that you have been wronged. When he tried it, Walter was once again taking on a force even more determined than himself, the British Army. The solution was as simple as it was cruel and horrific. Force feeding. Norval was pinioned by a couple of soldiers, a tube was put down his throat and a life-sustaining fluid poured down it with all the finesse of someone pouring petrol into a car that has run out of fuel. A realist like Walter soon went back to the knife and fork.

No matter that Walter played down the experience of force feeding. After all, even in his seventies and still fighting fit, he had a hard man image to burnish and maintain – it was a pretty grim affair. And if the person being force fed resisted and struggled it became downright dangerous and there are tales of victims choking to death. Incidentally, Norval credits one reason for his longevity and health to many years in prison. He points out that the food, however unexciting, was nutritious enough and, of course, there was no access to the demon drink. Sleep and rest was part of a regular routine. And in his day drugs behind prison bars was not the problem that it is now. There was also the bonus of regular workouts in the gym and on the prison football field. Inside for long years, he picked up the exercise habit and to this day likes a daily workout with the weights.

Even in the toughest of jails there is a humour that helps make doing time slightly less mindnumbingly boring. Walter

Norval, widely acknowledged as Glasgow's first Godfather of Crime, once shared a sojourn in Barlinnie with Arthur Thompson Snr, his successor and the man labelled by noted crime writer Reg McKay as 'The Last Godfather'.

Thompson, always a scary figure to meet outside in any circumstance, indulged his cruel sense of humour in one prank. The grapevine informed him that a fellow inmate had an Achilles heel. This guy was a bully, adept with the 'chib', who could hold his own with the toughest blade merchants of the slums. Even a gun pointing at his head would probably have been swatted aside. But he had a paranoid fear of rats and mice. And he was sure that Barlinnie was full of fearsome rodents hungry for a nibble at him. In fact, mice and rats, despite the desperate conditions the prisoners endured in the late forties, were not a problem. If there had been any rats in the place they would have thought they were in paradise because in those days the inmates slept on mattresses on wooden frames just a few inches off the floor. Ideal for a rodent wanting to chew on a two-legged rat.

This guy's obvious fear of rats gave Thompson – perhaps feeling deprived of the pleasure of scaring anyone he met as was his wont on the outside – the chance of a little evil-minded power play. One day a bit of an old scrubbing brush was found. With a length of cord attached to it, the brush was inserted into a bit of piping near the cell of the Man Who Hated Rats. A careful tug or two on the cord produced a nice little scratching sound that had the victim leaping onto the table in his cell and screaming blue murder for the warders to rescue him from the rats obviously bent on invading his cell. It provided splendid entertainment for the hardhearted cons, some of whom, you suspect, would have eaten a rat sandwich with relish.

Despite the occasional prank and a rough and ready make-the-most-of-it sense of humour, a deep sadness pervades the atmosphere in any penal establishment. The humour, such as it is, has to be put into context. If you spend 168 hours a week behind bars the time passed in a humorous way is tiny. But it is there and it is inventive. One expert on the subject was Robbie Glen, an ex-deputy governor who is a brilliant after-dinner speaker. Robbie once had an altercation with a tabloid which was surprisingly touchy about some of his humorous tales of life in the jail. But Robbie in my view was always laughing *with* the prisoners rather than at them. As is the case with most prison humour.

Incidentally William McIlvanney based his story 'The Prisoner' in his book of short stories entitled *The Walking Wounded* on him after he visited Robbie at Dungavel. Robbie's humour is illustrated in a little flyer publicising his second career as an after-dinner speaker when he points out, referring to himself, that: 'In his youth he played junior football professionally but his career was cut short tragically at an early age due to lack of ability. He still holds the Lanarkshire Schoolboy 440 yards record, because it's now gone metric!' Robbie got many cracking reviews for his speechmaking, the *Sunday Times* going so far as to say of Robbie, 'this man should carry a government health warning, he is seriously funny'. Robbie has a profoundly handicapped daughter and he developed a walking aid for her with his staff and prisoners in 1981 which is now being used in 41 hospitals and schools in Scotland to teach handicapped children how to walk.

All prisoners endure hour after hour of boredom and almost endless thoughts of nothing but your current predicament and, perhaps, for the more thoughtful, how you ended up in a tough prison. The perception of some of those on the outside is that prisoners live in a kind of cosseted atmosphere with regular meals, flat-screen TVs in a sort of home from home. That is a fantasy. Even in modern Barlinnie in 2011 it would be fairer to make a comparison with the Bangkok Hilton rather than the Glasgow Hilton.

A fairly usual way for prisoners to ease the endless boredom of confinement is to let their mind wander into complex plans for escape. And escapes can happen in any prison, no matter how efficient. But they are the exception rather than the rule. And they usually end up in a swift recapture. Glasgow can be a hard place to hide and the reappearance of a villain on his own patch gets the underworld talking. Les Brown, one of Glasgow's most legendary and successful detectives, told me of an amusing escape and recapture he was involved in. Les always had top contacts in the underworld and was often in a position to predict what would happen before it did. Such was the case with John 'Mad Dog' Duggan in the eighties. Les learned from a man in police custody that Duggan was going to escape from the Bar-L with the help of an Andy Steele. As any detective would do, he phoned to warn the Governor of the time, Mr McKenzie, about the planned escape. The Governor took it calmly – he seemed to have more faith in his prison's security than Duggan had.

But at three in the morning Les got a message to call the prison. The 'Mad Dog' – a nickname that never seems to go out of fashion – had somehow removed the bars from his cell window, climbed on to the roof, and then, moving hand over hand, had used telephone and other wires to climb on to the gatehouse roof. But he had a surprise when he jumped to the ground outside the prison. There was no sight or sound of the pre-arranged getaway car – his friends had given him a dizzy. There was nothing for it but simply to leg it away from the scene as fast as he could.

Mr McKenzie may have taken the original warning calmly, but now he was angry and he wanted Duggan back. About a week later Les got a call from Duggan's wife. Hiding from the cops seemed not much better than being in the jail. Duggan now wanted to give himself up to Les and so the detective went with a colleague, Detective Sergeant Jim Montgomery, to the Duggan house in Possilpark. Mrs Duggan established that no one had had breakfast and the cops and their quarry sat down to a hefty fry up of bacon and eggs and all the trimmings. Inner man satisfied, the cuffs were snapped on Duggan and he was on his way back behind bars where, for sure, the breakfasts would not be of the same quality. Duggan went on to sample life in other Scottish jails including Peterhead where he caught a headline or two in one of the many rooftop riots in that troubled place. He was once seen holding a placard which read: 'Fuck Nelson Mandela – free me'.

Escapes are always in the back of the mind of everyone in the prison service. Sometimes bad luck and bad timing are important. Barlinnie's record is undoubtedly first class with regard to escapes, but there are always vulnerable points in any system. Once inside, even the most resourceful prisoner is hard put to beat the system. The danger time is when prisoners are moved around from court to prison or one prison to another. This was highlighted in October 1998 when the then governor, Roger Houchin, came under fire when two prisoners were mistakenly released in a two-week period.

This, of course, unleashed the twin attack packs of press and politicians. Mr Houchin had to react to aggressive questioning from the newspapers and reject any suggestion he should resign. He pointed out that the jail at that time had 75,000 movements in and out in a year. He said: 'It just happens that two quite unrelated incidents occurred in two weeks and I don't make excuses for that – they should not have happened.' And he pointed out that over the years the jail had maintained an enviable record with regard to security. One of the 'escapers' – though that adjective is a bit dramatic for an incident that did not involve an escape tunnel or even a picked lock – was re-arrested by the police after a few days and the other, who was liberated 'in error', later gave himself up to the authorities. A pretty minor event in the Barlinnie Story though it was enough for the then Scottish Home Affairs minister Henry McLeish to tell all and sundry that he 'was very angry'. When you are dealing with the detention of criminals you are only a tiny slip away from the front pages! Resign? Absolutely not, said Roger Houchin, and he stayed in the post for another three years.

Trips to the Bar-L were not infrequent for Les Brown and sometimes had a surprising twist. A criminal pal of Walter Norval's was being held there on one occasion and was a suspect in a killing in the Coventry area. The con was John McDuff and an English murder squad wanted to come north to interview him. It resulted in one of those little legal contretemps that can happen in any police force. Les went with his immediate boss at the time, a detective chief superintendent, to meet the English detective at the airport. In the car on the way to the prison Les learned for the first time that the murder squad man wanted to interview McDuff as a suspect. Les, a man with a good knowledge of the law, then announced to his boss and their passenger that the English officer would not be allowed to question the Bar-L inmate as a suspect. 'What a load of crap,' said the chief super, 'just drive the car.'

In the prison, and in the Governor's office, Bob Hendry greeted Les as an old friend. The detective from the south said without delay that he wanted to interview a prisoner, John McDuff, 'who is the main suspect in a murder I am investigating'. Les took a deep breath – he knew what was coming next. Governor Hendry said: 'Not in this prison, you're not. Under the Prisons Scotland Act it is not permissible. You can interview him as a witness, or you can parade him as a suspect, and you can charge him. But that is all.' Mr Hendry then offered the group a coffee and I have no reason to disbelieve that, as Les told me, it was his most enjoyable jolt of Java for a long long time. As they sipped, Les suggested that since McDuff had relations in England he could be moved there. That's what happened and in the end McDuff was eliminated from the murder inquiry.

The intelligent, literate lawbreaker can use his time inside for education or even turn to writing himself. The Barlinnie Special Unit, which is dealt with in its full complexity later in this book, at one stage had a magazine produced by the prisoners and it is interesting how much poetry it included, mostly raw, biting and sometimes bitter verse reflecting the anger against society of those locked away. This is not ten thousand golden daffodils stuff. Sometimes the urge to express yourself showed itself in song. Walter Norval, in mellow mood, once entertained me with a little ditty called 'Barlinnie Hotel' (the comparison with hotels sometimes seems as deeply seated in the cons as it does to those on the outside!). It went like this...

BARLINNIE HOTEL

In Glasgow's fair city,
There's flashy hotels,
They give board and lodgings,
To all the big swells,
But the greatest of all now,
Is still in full swing,

Five beautiful mansions,
Controlled by the King.
There's bars on the windows,
And bells on the door,
Dirty big guard beds,
Attached to the floor,
I know 'cause I've been there,
And sure I can tell,
There's no place on earth like
Barlinnie Hotel.

I was driven from the Sheriff,
And driven by bus,
Drove through the streets,
With a terrible fuss,
Drove through the streets,
Like a gangster at state,
And they never slowed up,
Till they got to the gate.
As we entered reception,
They asked me my name,
And asked me my address,
And the reason I came,
As I answered these questions,
A screw rang the bell,
It was time for my bath,
In the Barlinnie Hotel.

After my bath, I was dressed like a doll,
The screw said, 'Quick march,
Right into E-Hall'
As I entered my flowery,   [flowery dell = cell]

I looked round in vain,
To think that three years here,
I had to remain.
At breakfast next morning, I asked for an egg,
The screw must have thought,
I was pulling his leg,
For when he recovered, he let out a yell,
'Jailbirds don't lay eggs,
In the Barlinnie Hotel!'

The day came for me,
When I had to depart,
I was as sick as a dog,
With joy in my heart,
For the comfort was good,
And the service was swell,
But I'll never return
To Barlinnie Hotel.

The only possible retort to such a sentiment is – IF ONLY! Sadly the Barlinnie Hotel does a considerable degree of repeat business. Even with the same families. Former Governor Bill McKinlay told me of fathers, grandfathers and sons who were regular clients.

Barlinnie at one time held youngsters in the untried areas who, on conviction, would be sentenced to Polmont Borstal, near Falkirk. Some observers thought of Borstals as finishing schools for young criminals, academies for training for a life of crime. There, too, the urge to burst into poignant verse surfaced in 'The Borstal Song'. Interestingly, too, it touches on the idea of going straight when the doors finally open and an inmate is marched back on to the streets:

THE BORSTAL SONG

I'm a lad who done wrong,
Very wrong in his time,
It was company that led me astray.
And, like many a youth,
I was led into crime,
And to Borstal they sent me away.
I once got a job in a dockyard,
Beside some old pals that I know,
But while working one day,
My foreman did say,
'My lad you must pack up and go.
You're a jailbird I know,
So pack up and go,
For jailbirds we do not employ.'
I said, 'Give me a chance to be honest,
Give me a chance, won't you, please?
For if luck's in my way,
I may find it some day,
Cause I am out on my Ticket of Leave!'

As I observed in *Glasgow's Godfather*, such a ditty echoing round the walls in darkened dorms would bring a tear to a glass eye, to use the old Glasgow phrase. But it seems the poignancy and emotion such songs engendered was pretty transitory. Out of the cells it was not long before old ways returned. Repeat business was guaranteed whether it was Borstal or Barlinnie.

Incidentally these two prison songs are far from the only musical references to the Bar-L. Cambuslang Folk Band Piggery Brae raise a laugh from time to time on their travels with a little ditty that goes:

66

It's murder, michty murder, in the jail
Where they feed you bread and water
If you ask them fae a pail for a tinnie
They'll send ye tae Barlinnie
Oh, it's murder, michty murder in the jail

Talking to old lags you get all sorts of different reactions to the penal system and it seems the older they are the more they accept the way society treats lawbreakers. You will not hear many young yobs giving out that previously mentioned old mantra: 'If you do the crime, you do the time'. But in the past many doing a stretch in Barlinnie had no difficulty believing in that concept. I have even heard of career criminals doing a stretch for a crime they did not commit and accepting it with a degree of resignation, balancing it against the crimes they got away with! That sort of thinking fits in with the hierarchical system in prisons. The old lag likes to stay out of trouble and milk the system for any privileges that may be going.

The youngsters, filled with anger and resentment, some thirsting to get back to their girlfriends and families, some simply thirsting to get back to their old violent ways, are a different kettle of fish. These are the guys the officers have to fear. Lashing out at your captors rather than being concerned about why you were jailed in the first place is sometimes their first priority. For this reason the distribution of privileges to the well-behaved in prison is important. As is the system of grading. Walter Norval was Status One in military prison. In Barlinnie he was, for a spell, Category A.

On this occasion he was inside for bank robbery rather than assault or attempted murder. And that rankled, giving him a lifelong belief that on occasion the justice system put crimes against property on a higher level than crimes against people.

To be Category A you were judged to be a 'menace to society' and, of course, such status had an effect on your daily life in prison. Category A prisoners in the late forties were locked up all day except for a one-hour exercise period. Even when in their cell they were under constant observation. And the so-called exercise was taken walking round the first landing in circles after the ordinary cons who were deemed less dangerous had gone to work in the sheds making willow baskets or whatever. Incidentally, prisoners are conditioned always to turn left on leaving cells to ease congestion on the narrow metal alleyways. Meals were delivered to your cell, denying you the association of eating with the other cons, and no one was supposed to speak to you through the door. In case anyone did not realise you were a special case, and did not fully understand the menace to society you were, a huge letter A was affixed to your door.

The regulations are always a challenge to prisoners and Norval had many friends in Barlinnie keen to make his Category A incarceration a little more bearable. Some would take the risk of smuggling a paper through his door or even an illicit cup of tea. Some of his fellow inmates of the time were famous figures often making headlines in the Glasgow tabloids, such as Billy Fullerton, offspring of the founder of the Billy Boys, and Tony Smith. Of these two, Norval told me that 'both lads were 100 per cent genuine cons. The screws would shout to Tony and Billy to get away from my door, but the lads would just tell them to fuck off as they were talking to a friend!'

But it was the very prison system itself that was to end the Category A deprivation of Norval. Cons get used to a constant stream of visitors and folk they label callously as 'fucking do gooders'. Visiting dignitaries and folk interested in prison conditions and helping in the redemption rather than revenge stakes are a welcome and frequent sight.

Prison visitors play a vital role. On one occasion a group looking round the jail saw the strange sight of a solitary Norval plodding around the largely empty hall. One of the dignitaries, an MP no less, did not like what he saw. And when the visiting group sat down later to discuss what they had seen, he asked some awkward questions about the treatment of the lone walker. To this enlightened politician it seemed that the Category A criminal was already being punished for his crimes without the extra punishment of being segregated from the other villains.

Within minutes, Norval was ordered down to the desk where a warder asked what would now be called a no-brainer: 'Do you want to mix with the others in the shed and be able to have your meals in the dining area with your friends?' The question did not need to be asked twice. The incident illustrates the power of an MP and the importance of regular prison visiting and inspections by people not professionally involved in the system.

The removal of Category A status allowed Norval to find himself in the work sheds and in the company of such villains and old associates from Maryhill as Barney Noon and Billie and Vinnie Manson. But if the Godfather had expected this to lead to a quiet life with his old criminal mates he was wrong. Pretty soon there was a knock on the door and he was bundled into a car heading north for further hardship in Peterhead. Incidentally, he had a spell in the dog boxes in Peterhead at the end of the journey.

Another noted Barlinnie potential Cat A prisoner was Paul Ferris. In 2000 he was doing time in the south but was sent up to Barlinnie for a brief spell to catch up on some accumulated family visits. He tells the story in *Vendetta*, a highly readable true crime book written with Reg McKay. As a potential escaper Ferris was not told in advance the actual date of his visit. So when he was roughly wakened one morning he had only time to snatch a few belongings before beginning the trip north. He threw a few things, including a book he had been given by a fellow prisoner, into a holdall and jumped when the officers said jump. The book he took with him was Dostoevsky's *The Brothers Karamazov*. The con who had passed it on recommended it as the best crime novel he had ever read. This could have raised the alarm bell of a wind up, but Paul Ferris knew that the donor of the book was a highly educated somewhat intellectual Irish nationalist who was behind bars for his politically motivated actions. Ferris tried hard to come to terms with the works of the Russian literary legend. He couldn't make it. Bloody hard going, was his review.

By this time Barlinnie did not have accommodation for Cat A prisoners and Ferris was held in the segregation unit known since the days of the Special Unit as the Wendy House. This meant no free association with the other prisoners and 23-hour lock ups every day. He knew some of the others on the wing and as they moved around to showers and the visiting room they had short conversations with each other. In an observation on this Ferris remarks in *Vendetta*: 'On earlier occasions in the Wendy House I would have received a bollocking from the screws for such breaches of the rules, but this time they were more relaxed and treated inmates with respect. It resulted in a trouble-free zone. Why can't all prisons learn that?'

Whatever the validity of such advice from hardened cons, Ferris was asked in one of these conversations if he had any books to read. Ferris did have a bundle of books by his favourite crime novelist, James Ellroy. He was not inclined to hand these over. Instead he told the young inmate he had been talking to that he had a cracker – 'the best crime novel I have ever read'. 'Brilliant,' the young guy replied. The Dostoevsky was duly handed over to a prison officer, as was required by the rules, to be passed to the unsuspecting young con. Anything that keeps the mind in gear in solitary is given a chance. So the recipient of the literary gift opened the pages and read. Each time Ferris met this guy in the wing he asked how he was getting on. To begin with he was told 'great' but at a subsequent meeting it was admitted that, 'I am finding it a bit hard going.'

Paul Ferris, playing the role of literary advisor, urged him to press on and told his pal that after a few hundred pages or so it became easier. The young con persisted. But as Ferris tells: 'About ten days after I had passed over *The Brothers Karamazov* I was lying out in my bunk totally engrossed in some really good novel. The whole wing was in total silence when "Ferris, you dirty rotten c***!" rang out. Page two hundred plus had been reached, as had the realization that it just did not get any easier. His fellow inmate had lost the plot, literally, and knew that he had had the piss taken out of him.

In a letter back to his IRA friend in the English jail, Ferris recounted the tale and got a letter back to say that the original donor had also struggled with the book! Apparently the book is still doing the rounds of prisons with the well-worn recommendation, 'the best crime novel I have ever read . . .' Maybe some day in some jail some con in solitary confinement will give Dostoevsky's tale of spiritual drama and moral struggle the same credit as such as Albert Einstein and Sigmund Freud, both admirers of the Russian masterpiece. Or maybe not.

Ferris also gives some insight into prison visiting. He remarks that meeting a close family member in jail was a hard reminder that he was locked up, a slap in the face about what he could not do to help those he loved. He took a week to get over every visit. I suspect that many in jail have similar feelings. It is a big part of the punishment.

Ferris and his version of life in Barlinnie featured in one of the most famous trials in Scottish criminal history. In the end Paul Ferris 'walked' – as the city's criminals like to describe a trial that sees the accused released. In 1992 Ferris, then a baby-faced 28-year-old, and looking for all the world like a successful businessman without a care in the world, stood trial in Glasgow's High Court charged with killing Arthur Thompson Jnr and also accused of six drugs and violence charges. The trial ran for 54 days and was at the time the longest-running murder trial in Scottish criminal history, with unofficial estimates putting the cost at £750,000. More than 300 witnesses were cited in a trial that was said to have every ingredient – sex, drugs, humour, violence, love and tragedy. The humour, some of it in Barlinnie, interests us, but right away it must be said that Paul Ferris left the court a free man, found not guilty on all charges and able to stand at the top of the court steps posing for newspaper and television photographers before taking perhaps the most famous of all 'walks' back into the dark world he had inhabited.

Hundreds of thousands of words were spoken at the trial, keeping eight shorthand reporters so busy that you suspect some might have had a claim for repetitive strain injury knocking around at the back of their minds. Keeping track of what was going on was a mammoth task. One *Herald* reporter alone was said to have filled 40 notebooks. Despite the gravity of the charges, laughter in court was not infrequent. The evidence of some of the witnesses occasioned hilarity. Commenting on the testimony of one woman who had given evidence, a witness told the court that she was an alcoholic and at the time she 'spoke to the polis she was not compos mental'.

The *Herald* diary, famed for seeing the humorous side of life, did a roaring trade in tales from the trial. One of the best allowed it to award what it called The Most Abrupt Change of Evidence

Award to a hardened criminal who described a fellow villain as 'not a very nice' person. Asked to clarify his remark he immediately replied: 'He is a fucking toerag.'

At times even the judge, the legendary Lord McCluskey, found it hard to resist a smile. When told that a witness had decided, in some haste, to go down the coast to Irvine on holiday, without any luggage, he inquired incredulously: 'Didn't he bring a beach towel?' And he also got involved in an exchange with Ferris about goings on in the Barlinnie segregation unit. There, it seemed, the prisoners had a passion for chess, that age-old test of intellect, and played by shouting moves from their cells to each other. One newspaper reported that Ferris, already the possessor of full hard man status, gained admiration for his mental prowess by winning £500 in one move. Trial reports said that at one point the judge became quite engrossed in the finer points of the move called 'castling', something that Ferris had apparently been explaining to his fellow prisoner. Such is life in the Bar-L. At times.

5

DIRTY CUPS AND
FINDING GOD BEHIND BARS

The reign of Queen Victoria was marked by what the history books usually describe as 'a growing humanitarianism' and some would say that Barlinnie was an expression of such a process. It was designed to alleviate horrible overcrowding in Her Majesty's Prisons in Glasgow. The fact that it ended up with more prisoners than it was designed for, almost from day one, is regrettable, but it should not be allowed to obscure the visionary thinking of its builders. The Victorian era put great weight on the Christian religion and values. Just how seriously the subjects of the Queen took their faith is evident in the church inside the walls of the prison. It came into use in the 1880s shortly after the five great halls began to be filled by assorted villains pulled from the streets of Glasgow and sentenced for their crimes to confinement in the Bar-L.

Today the church, almost at the centre of the whole complex of cellblocks, health centre and workshops, is still remarkably impressive. The images of imprisonment are largely unseen, with no iron bars and generally no clanking of keys in locks. It is as like a church in a prosperous suburb as makes no difference. Though, curiously, there is a shortage of stained glass. Today it is used for worship by several different faiths and also as a theatre space for performance and events by groups from within the prison and outsiders giving the occasional concert or other entertainment. Sitting in this extraordinary and exceptional church it seems to be almost haunted by the shades of the men, and at one time women, who worshipped here – a disparate group, unreformed hard men using the Kirk as a brief escape from the cells, prisoners who had found faith during their incarceration, men days away from the gallows and prison staff of a religious disposition.

Religion plays a big role in prison where the long lonely hours are inductive of deep thought. Men locked away from their fellows for years have time to consider their life and their ways. Many, of course, do not give a jot – their only concern is to get out from behind bars and back on the streets to resume old ingrained lawless ways. Others, with much time to reflect, take to religion, or maybe resume any religious notions they had in younger, saner days. And the ministers of religions who visit the jail are in great demand to interpret what concerns of conscience, or no conscience, a prisoner has. Men of the cloth are welcomed generally, although in its early days the Special Unit was a chaplain-free zone. In particular, chaplains can be of great help to youngsters preparing for release. A friendly face in a dog collar, one of the many part-time visiting chaplains, stands out from the youngsters in coloured sweatshirts and jeans, the lads 'who have dun wrong', as the old prison song has it.

And Barlinnie, perhaps more than any other Scottish prison, has a great history of men of faith working with the inmates to rehabilitate even the hardest of hard tickets – godfathers of a different kind from your Arthur Thompsons and Walter Norvals. The first full-time chaplain, Bill Christman, is a Barlinnie legend. He had an unconventional background for such a job. He was born not in Glasgow where most of the Barlinnie inmates breathe their first, but in Joplin, Missouri. His first job was as a salesman in a record shop specializing in rhythm and blues, not too difficult a task in such an area. But this remarkable man was not destined to spend his life behind the counter in a music store. A summer holiday break in West Virginia 'where poverty was so dreadful it turned my values upside-down' was followed by a slow recovery from a bout of pneumonia which provided time to think about life and values. He took the major step of deciding to study religion and here the chance that was to change his life played a part. A friend mentioned Edinburgh and its prestigious place in the world of religion and the idea of studying abroad appealed to the man from Missouri. One big advantage, he figured, was that if after a while in Scotland's capital he lost the urge to study and continue in religion he could return home to the States causing the minimum of ripples in his life. And he would have had the character shaping advantage of working abroad.

But, of course, Bill Christman stayed the course and graduated. He found himself ministering in Niddrie, one of the capital's most depressed areas. Four years later he went back across the Atlantic on a prestigious scholarship to Harvard. But Scotland was his destiny. And he got a call to come back as minister in Easterhouse, down the road from Barlinnie. This was a parish with problems involving crime and poverty, but the area also had its share of decent folk doing their best for their families in difficult conditions.

Bill Christman decided to accept the challenge. All that was missing was the airfare. But his fellow students had a whip-round to solve that problem. 'Maybe they wanted rid of me,' he joked. He was to spend seven years in Easterhouse at a time when the area's gangs were getting maximum exposure in the local press. The scheme was, like others in Glasgow, the result of well-meaning thinking by the then Glasgow Corporation. Easterhouse, Castlemilk, Drumchapel and the like were what became known in the city as 'outer circle' schemes. Acknowledging the squalor of many of the city centre housing areas, huge new schemes, some with the population of places like Perth, were thrown up on green field sites in record time. The houses were fine, inside toilets and all mod cons. The trouble was the authorities neglected to provide, until many years later, civilised facilities like libraries, swimming pools, churches, pubs and restaurants. The result was what one comedian called 'deserts wi windaes'. And crime became a major problem in such areas with the police shorthanded – at one stage a couple of coppers on bikes were responsible for policing a population of more than 40,000 in Castlemilk – and stretched to maintain law and order among those decamped from the city. The new housing stock was a huge step forward from the hundreds of inner city homes that were barely fit for human habitation. But these older areas at least had some sense of community and history.

Bill Christman and his ideas got on fine in Easterhouse and there were successes. Maybe his accent helped him with the locals – he said that it was by now 'half American hillbilly and half Easterhouse'. At one stage he was running five football teams for young gang members, or potential members. This valiant attempt to show aimless youngsters that there was more to life than violence and aggression was on the whole pretty successful and Bill was able to tell an interviewer that: 'Only one boy in any of those teams ever got into more trouble.'

The next stop in a fascinating career was a move to the douce Lansdowne Church in the prosperous, bohemian, at least for Glasgow, area of the West End. But there were challenges here, too. Challenges that may have helped a prison chaplain in the years ahead. In the West End the challenge was, with the help of the congregation, 'trying to build multi-faith bridges within a community'. The next stop was another testing challenge – a move to St Columba's in the Firth of Clyde seaside resort of Ayr. This was a new congregation created by the merging of three churches and a different set of problems. His seaside sojourn ended when he heard about the new Kirk post of full-time prison chaplain at Barlinnie, the huge edifice that had played such a dominant role in his life in Easterhouse. He applied, got the job and was on the move again, remarking, 'At each post along the way I learned something that matters.'

So an American man of God became the Church of Scotland's first full-time prison chaplain. Whether visiting the Bar-L or any other Scottish prison, Bill had a golden rule for his new role: 'Regardless of what the crime involved is, I don't want to know the details of why any man or woman was sent to prison before I meet them. I am human like anyone else and could be prejudiced and that is something I must try hard to avoid.' Bill, who had acquired the nickname 'the Godfather' in his previous existence in Easterhouse, saw his new role as supporter of the long established part-time chaplains. One of his most valuable roles was visiting family members of prisoners when a prisoner told him of his worries. One of the saddest things that happens to a prisoner is when letters from loved ones outside the walls stop coming. The prisoner is left in the dark about what is happening to his nearest and dearest, his imagination running riot. It is a particularly unpleasant form of mental torture. At times like these the chaplain is the natural, and often correct person to turn to.

Sorting out such matters was all in the day's work for a man

DIRTY CUPS AND FINDING GOD BEHIND BARS

who liked to mix and talk in the streets with late-night people. Bill so often got to the scene of street trouble first that one chief constable gave him a card to carry to show to any inquiring constable on the beat exactly who he was. Handy, too, when he ran a soup kitchen in George Square. Along with his Roman Catholic colleagues, Bill and the other chaplains had to work within the rules and regulations of the prison service and to preserve a total confidentiality. One interviewer told him that sometimes a prisoner would see the chaplain as a soft touch and asked, 'Are you one?' He got a devastatingly truthful response: 'Maybe sometimes, but so often there can be a hidden reason why a prisoner seeks your help and you've got to find what might be there.'

One of the many who found salvation in Barlinnie was Bill McGibbon, who graduated from gangland to the God squad. Religion came more directly into his life rather than at the direct intervention of a chaplain. He served a stretch after being sent down for attempted murder. One night in the loneliness of the great prison he dreamed that one day when he was at last a free man he would return to the prison to spread the word of God among the hundreds of Godless inmates. So it happened and in 1993 he told his story of returning to tell hard cases that 'Jesus loves them – even if their mothers don't.' Bill was a founding member of the Scottish Offenders project, a group that bought a flat in Glasgow's Southside to help reha- bilitate ex-prisoners, particularly released lifers who faced all sort of problems when finally outside after years in jail.

Bill McGibbon, a remarkable character, had grown up in Bridgeton in the east end where many of the locals were regu- lars in the Bar-L and where in those days the razor gangs ran wild. Although he had day jobs in the meat market and work in a shipyard at night he still found time to run with the infamous Baltic Fleet and Brigton Derry. Not a man to mince words or hide his history, he told one Glasgow reporter that 'your razor went everywhere with you.' Though he credits that dream in the cells as a turning point, the influence of prison chaplains was also in play – his conversion to a life in the service of religion had begun with Bible classes in the Bar-L. Years of working to convert others who had gone down the wrong track in life followed.

Surprising as it is to someone with no experience of life in jail as has been remarked earlier, there are more smiles behind bars than you would expect. The chaplains get a fair share of humour from the inmates they befriend. A joke shared is a good joke. The *Herald* diary has printed some classics over the years. One involved Father Jim Lawlor, one of the Roman Catholic chaplaincy team at the prison. Father Lawlor was visiting a youngster recently admitted. It was obvious the youngster was not too comfortable to be visited by a priest, but in an effort to put him at his ease Father Jim asked him his age. 'I'll be seventeen in two weeks,' was the answer. 'Oh,' said the priest, 'that means we are both Capricorns'. 'Not me,' said the new inmate – 'I am a protestant!'

One of the great religious characters in the Barlinnie story was Father Willy Slavin who spent ten years as the prison's Catholic chaplain as well as making waves in the newspapers as a long-distance cyclist and co-coordinator of the Scottish Drugs Forum. To this day no one has known more about prisons and drugs than Father Slavin. He was outspoken about society's continuing habit of the courts filling prisons with addicts who he believed needed help rather than being banged up. Thankfully his thinking has now, to a certain extent, been acted on. There are still too many addicts behind bars, but now at least they can get some help from 'in house' medical experts and the facilities of a well-equipped health centre behind the walls.

On admission, drug problems are assessed in depth. Father Slavin was at odds in the early nineties with the Scottish Office on whether or not the Scottish Prison Service was doing enough to tackle drug addiction behind bars. And that, no matter the improvements recently, will always be a contentious issue. Can enough ever be done?

One Kirk chaplain, Alex Wilson, a cheery man who walks the walk inside the walls and seems to know everyone from inmates to staff, introduced me to another man who is a legendary part of Barlinnie history. Eddie Simpson is a tall, courteous Church of Scotland minister with a ready smile and that great attribute to anyone working in a prison – a huge sense of humour. That comes out as you talk to him, as does his sense of compassion and reality. Eddie Simpson is a minister of the Kirk who knows the score, and his fellow man, after a quarter of a century or so as a part-time chaplain in the Bar-L. A first-name type of guy, Eddie was the minister in Giffnock South, a parish miles away from the east end in distance in what some could think of as another world. But not Eddie, who was as at home with the hard cases in the Bar-L as he was with the businessmen and women of the southside. He served God with equal dedication in different ways in both places.

Eddie Simpson first walked through the fearsome main gate in '83, requested by the Kirk to take on the role of part-time chaplain. It wasn't the most popular job, but he accepted the challenge. Apart from a couple of visits when he was ministering in rural Ayrshire, in the pleasant seaside town of Girvan, he barely knew the prison. It was a much different place then – now the warders are carers as well as keepers, and reassuringly for a man of the cloth, redemption seems to be winning that eternal prison battle over revenge or retribution. At least on points. But back in the eighties, before the troubles with rooftop riots had spawned a new strategy in Scotland's prisons called Fresh Start, many of the prison officers were ex-military with little training who walked in the footsteps of men, with notable exceptions, who were basically the 'key men' of the old-style prisons. To them the custodial duties took priority over any caring aims.

When Eddie started, to say the regime was much harsher would be masterly understatement. When he thinks back he remembers one odd little aspect of life in the days when prisoners had no access to phones to keep in touch with families, no television to relieve some of the colossal boredom, and little in the way of training for release or encouragement to turn your life around. One of the first indignities inflicted on the newly convicted was that your watch, if you had one, was taken from you and nowhere in the five huge halls was there a clock. On visiting a cell Eddie remembers the almost inevitable question was 'Hullo boss, what's the time?' The lack of clocks in the jail is interesting. Is it because the inmates should not be reminded of the time and how slowly it can pass? I doubt it – that other iconic prison, Alcatraz, had in its heyday a huge clock that could be seen from most of the cells. Indeed the American cons incarcerated on the island in San Francisco bay called the area where the clock was 'Times Square', to remind them of the buzz in the Big Apple.

Another memory of the bad old days in Barlinnie is that each cell had a coloured card on the door – white for Protestants, green for Catholics and pink for Anglicans, all anachronistic in these multi-faith days. Eddie also remembers in the early years the banging on cell doors and screaming. It was a nightmarish sound that went on almost constantly and could be heard even outside the doors of the huge halls. No TV – or methadone – in cells in those days to calm and occupy the imprisoned. There was also the loathsome task, swept into history with the end of slopping out, of the morning ritual of the 'bomb squads' who went round the outside walls of the halls picking up the excrement wrapped in newspaper thrown out the windows of cells where the chamber pots were full to overflowing.

Perhaps it is the overdose of 'thinking time' that prison gives, but many prisoners, not just the 60 to 80 or so who turn up for the Sunday Kirk service, are troubled souls who seek advice on spiritual matters, sometimes more directly than a Giffnock resident might approach the problem. Eddie tells of a guy in his seventies, a Bar-L regular well known to the Chaplain, who knocked on his door one day and said that, now he was growing old, maybe he should find out something about his Maker. The Gideon Bible is a reading staple in prisons, too, with many inmates asking for a copy of the version specially prepared for prison use. This little book has a preamble telling how it should be used. It lists emotions like sadness, feeling low, shame, guilt, regret, depression, etc, and points the reader to passages in the scriptures that might help. Eddie recalls one sad youngster saying to him, 'Where do I start? I've got every effing one of them.' Meetings of prison groups, interested enough to talk over religious and other prison matters, can be a bit different to Bible classes or scripture study on the outside.

The coffee and biscuits are similar, but the mores a little different. Eddie had a prisoner friend who attended such meetings and helped out with the coffees. But he was a little economical with the washing-up liquid. It was good enough for him to 'sine' out the mugs with a quick splash under the tap. A tad more fastidious, Eddie asked the inmate to make sure his was washed properly. The host went off to the kettle in the meeting room kitchen and returned with a tray of steaming coffees and a plate of custard creams and politely asked, 'Who wanted the clean cup?'

That 80 or so – sometimes it's more, sometimes less – who attend the Kirk's Sunday morning services is a creditable number when you consider there is a separate Roman Catholic mass and that the Muslims have their own religious services. And the Bar-L congregation is not bolstered, as it is outside, with wives and children. In percentage terms it is pretty good. The Catholic chaplains and Kirk ministers cooperate fully with shared services at Christmas and Easter and in the daily ministering to the needs of the inmates.

The church behind the walls is unique in the prison. It is, for instance, the only place where those in the segregation unit, sometimes there for offences against children – the so-called 'beasts' of the jail – can mingle with the other convicts, though there are always some officers in the background. Services are seldom interrupted. Eddie does recall one dramatic little episode of the kind unlikely to occur in most kirks. One Sunday a prisoner, a hard ticket noted for rooftop escapades in the past, took it upon himself to clamber on top of the furniture and climb up towards the roof to hide in the rafters. The service went on as if nothing had happened. And at the close the climber was hauled back down by the officers and taken to his cell. He apologised to the chaplain the next day. Just another incident in prison life!

The chaplains of different faiths also share the job of interviewing new arrivals to offer them any help and understanding they can at one of the most traumatic moments in a prisoner's life. This shared duty can mean that a rabid Orangeman can meet a Roman Catholic priest as his first insight into religion in the prison. But even that seldom produces any bad feeling; it is normally just accepted.

Every prisoner has a right to a visit from a member of his faith – Protestants, Catholics, rastas, Muslims, Mormons whatever. This is the main task of the full-time Kirk minister and four part-time chaplains. There are also three Catholic priests, one nun, and one Muslim Imam on call. After a night in the First Night centre, a relatively new and humane initiative designed to ease some of the shock at beginning a sentence, the chaplains play a role in the induction process meeting that explains, particularly to first timers, how the system works. This is a really valuable tool in defusing tension in the prison. The cons know their rights inside the prison and the rules are clear. If they want to write a letter, or sadly a too often occurrence, have someone write one for them, or if they want a chaplain to visit or to make a complaint, they know who to turn to.

The chaplains are in demand when prisoners have problems at home, particularly bereavements. Even here there can be a touch of humour. One minister commiserating with an inmate on the loss of a family member who had committed suicide, asked politely what had happened, to be told the deceased 'had taken a bad turn'. The cons can get close to the 'God squad'. On one occasion Father Larry McMann was talking in the prison about a recent break-in at the priests' home where he stayed. 'Talk to the boys about it,' someone suggested, 'they might be able to help.' So Father Larry duly recounted his story to a group of guys, not unfamiliar with the break-in scene in Glasgow, giving them the sordid details and in particular bemoaning the loss of a nearly new Toshiba DVD player. The cons listened carefully, no doubt considering what they could do about this outrage. And as the priest walked away from their chat one shouted out: 'Does it have to be a Toshiba?'

Eddie, too, has had more than his share of laughs. Once he was in a cell discussing a matter of concern which was that the prisoner had wanted to donate his body to medical science. During this chat the con's cellmate lay faking sleep, and lack of concern about the conversation, with a blanket over his face. One of the prisoner's worries was that his body was 'not in good enough shape' to be of use. At this the cellmate was interested enough to remove the blanket and remark, 'I telt him to try McKellar (the famous maker of sausages).'

But behind the rough and ready everyday humour, the chaplains face the reality of dealing with and trying to make sense of hundreds of wasted lives. Eddie Simpson is saddened that in these so-called enlightened days of the twenty-first century, many of the young inmates of Barlinnie arrive pasty-faced, under fed, ravaged by drink or drugs, just boys who have often never been more than a few miles from their slum home, boys who have never been on a plane or holidayed in fresh air and sunshine. Boys from broken homes who have never had parental love or concern. His worries echoed that of the famous minister Cameron Peddie who, in the forties, valiantly tried to help the disadvantaged youth of the Gorbals and often remarked how 'sickly' many of them were. Peddie thought some of his boys even relished a stay in the Bar-L for the advantages of regular meals and regular exercise. Eddie Simpson and his colleagues have, as one of their tasks, to maintain any feelings in those who have least some experience of religious awareness and install in those who have none at least a smidgeon of interest in matters of conscience. Anyone who has contacts with lawbreakers knows that a simple lack of conscience, as experienced by most people, is often totally missing in the offender.

They don't do conscience. They care nothing of what their criminal acts do to other people.

Eddie illustrates this with the story of one Barlinnie regular. On the outside he lives in fine style in a suburban bungalow, drives the inevitable four-by-four, holidays abroad and never ventures out without a thick wallet. All financed by crime, mostly non-violent. This guy is completely without conscience. His logic is that in thirty years or so of this type of crime he has 'only' done four years in jail. On release he will resume his old lifestyle. No doubt about it. He reckons the time inside is worth it, balanced against his lifestyle while free. And in any case it might be years before he is 'collared' again. Quite a challenge for any chaplain.

The conscience issue also popped up some years ago when the Department of Accounting and Finance at Glasgow University pioneered an optional course for accounting degree students devoted to the study of accounting ethics and the development of ethical sensibility. Course leader Ken McPhail said: 'Qualified accountants are disturbingly ill-equipped to respond to the challenges of the new business environment. Students are not provided with an understanding of where accounting fits into the broader political economy or the critical and ethical skills that will be required to respond to the changing role for accounting in the new business environment.'

Perceptive stuff when you look at it in the context of the recent collapse of the banking system and the ethics, or lack of them, of the so-called Masters of the Universe who ran the banks into the ground with greed and inefficiency. Part of the university course included a visit to Barlinnie in an experiment to see if the location where students experienced ethics education had any impact on the way they engaged with social issues. It would also be a sharp reminder that business crime could end up with the accountant behind bars. It also helped illustrate how business decisions affect people's lives.

The students right away got some practicalities – numbers are important in a prison: numbers in and out, visitors, inmates and staff are regularly counted. If there is a discrepancy, everything is shut down until the account balances. Less theoretical was a visit to the cells. Slopping out prevailed at that time, and the three-foot-square dog boxes for holding prisoners were still in use, and the young visitors were suitably horrified. One prison officer dealt with the conscience issue by pointing out that many inmates treat other individuals as objects and many cannot see they have done anything wrong. The study group, the university reported, 'was able to relate this to the problem of objectification within accounting and business and how treating individuals as objects – as categories like wages and expenses – make it easier for accountants to treat them in an unethical manner.' This was not the normal sort of 'education' dispensed inside the walls of the Bar-L. But as recent events have shown, giving a conscience to the 'bean counters' is no bad idea.

Eddie Simpson is concerned about the levels of methadone necessarily prescribed to the prison population. His comment on the drug is, 'I hate it.' But considering the abuse of drugs out of jail by the inmates, the temptation of smuggling the stuff into it and the on-going addiction problems, it is not a problem that is going to go away, nor one with an easy solution.

Also of concern to Eddie is the notion of many not involved in prison work that the solution to violent crime, indeed any form of crime, is to lock 'em up and throw away the key. He thinks the general public has got to learn that prison must be made to work for our society. A regime that does not have redemption at its heart, whether or not in the full religious sense, is bound to fail and fail at a huge cost to society. Unreformed prisoners on release simply go back into their old ways and society pays the cost of increased security, more policing, higher insurance premiums, fear of burglary or attack in the streets. It is in everyone's interest to make the prison experience something that cuts down re-offending and it is not just the concern of those dismissed as do-gooders. Everyone benefits when prison works. The role of the prison chaplains may not be something that gets much media exposure. But there can be no more rewarding job than trying to give a sense of self worth back to men and boys who have reached a physical and emotional nadir. Prison governors down the decades owe a great debt to their chaplains. And so does society.

6

DOG BOXES, CHAMBER POTS AND COMPENSATION

Barlinnie is a place of many adjectives. If 'iconic' is indeed the word most apt to describe the place in general terms and 'sensational' the natural way to describe the various attacks on staff, rooftop riots and assorted exercise yard rumbles down the year,s then 'disgusting' and 'degrading' are the only words for one prison practice now thankfully swept away: slopping out. But to remove this blot on the penal system took many years, much money paid to lawyers, much time in court and much hand wringing by politicians. For anyone who has been on holiday on Planet Zog for the past ten years or so and not aware what was going on, the practice of slopping out can be simply explained – lock away a couple of prisoners in a tiny cell for ten hours or so with no access to toilets, hand washing, clean towels or disinfectant and let them defecate and urinate in front of each other into what are essentially buckets. If that is not enough of a torture, let the vile smell from an individual prisoner's cell mix with the stench from dozens of others during the long nights locked up.

Before taking a look at this practice and how it was finally ended it is important to say that the prison staff, too, suffered from a regime that allowed slopping out to go on for so long.

And that in the whole sorry story it seems that what the staff suffered in administering the slopping out routines has been largely ignored. The prisoners grabbed most of the headlines. But it was the prisoners who benefited financially – as well as in terms of hygiene – from the change in policy that eventually put toilets into every cell. The effect on staff – not exactly high earners for the most part – seems to have been swept under the figurative carpet.

Even if most of the headline coverage of slopping out featured the effect on inmates, it should not be forgotten that it was the officers who had to supervise the emptying of buckets into foul smelling drains morning after morning. As one joked to me, a regular issue of clothes pegs, noses for the use of, would have been appropriate.

The award of financial compensation for the damage caused by slopping out to one prisoner, Robert Napier, sparked claims galore from inmates, but it did also provoke the prison officers themselves to consider that their human rights had been breached by supervising and watching the slopping out process. It was worked out by the Prison Officers Association that since the European Court of Human Rights was embodied in the Scottish Constitution in 1999, at least 2,000 people had had to work in prisons, including Barlinnie, where slopping out took place. The POA said staff had to endure degrading working conditions including daily exposure to the stench of human waste. Interestingly, slopping out had been banned in England and Wales as long ago as 1996. The anger of the Scottish officers, and their thirst for compensation, was no doubt partly fuelled by reports that at one stage the Scottish Prison Service had admitted that it had increased a fund to pay a flood of slopping out compensation claims from prisoners from £26m to £44m, a whacking 70% rise. They also made the point that the campaign to end the practice had been going on for at least 15 years and successive Labour and Tory governments had done nothing about it.

The anger of the officers was well represented by one spokesman of their union who said: 'It is a vile, reprehensible thing to witness. Staff have to stand near the basins watching people slop out and you can imagine what it is like first thing in the morning.' He went on: 'There have been lots of occasions when inmates would deliberately throw the contents at the prison warders. It is a degrading, horrible thing to happen to you.' It poses the thought that there are no comparable jobs where, in doing the bidding of society to protect it from criminals, you end up dodging buckets of faeces and urine thrown at you by violent criminals. Cash just doesn't compensate for that.

The whole issue had been under discussion for years. But a report in 2002 estimated that 1,900 prisoners in Scottish establishments were still slopping out. Peterhead was a particular problem because of the design of the prison and the materials used to build it. The next year the report on the inspection of Barlinnie painted a picture of conditions in the prison at that time. The report contained some plus points and highlighted the 'good relationships between staff and prisoners, and a determination by staff to cope with very high numbers.' But it pointed out that slopping out remained in two of the giant halls. It also underlined the fact that some prisoners were locked up for very long periods of time and many of the prisoners in the very bad conditions had not been convicted of a crime but were being held in Barlinnie on remand. The slopping out system is totally indefensible, but it seems almost beyond belief that just a handful of years ago men awaiting trial and therefore technically innocent should be subjected to such barbaric conditions.

Scotland's Chief Inspector of Prisons, Andrew McLellan, said that the prison had made progress since the last inspection, but despite significant investment, it had not yet changed enough.

Dr McLellan continued: 'Overcrowding and the issue of drugs, particularly the provision of medication, pervade much of the prison's work. This report makes a very positive assessment of much good work being carried out to deal with addiction problems.

'It also concludes that staff are determined to deal with the very high numbers, and not merely cope, but generally seek to develop relationships with prisoners which are relaxed and humane.

'However, some prisoners are still locked up for very long periods of time (sometimes up to 23 hours a day) in very poor conditions. Slopping out exists in two Halls and most of the prisoners who have no integral sanitation are also the victims of the chronic overcrowding: so nearly all of these prisoners are sharing a cell. The "holding" cubicles in Reception are not acceptable.' These are the cells the cons called dog boxes, though in reality no person with any decent instincts would even put a dog into them.

He went on to praise the efforts to make useful work accessible to the convicted prisoners in addition to good work on education and other aspects of the regime. The halls that had already been refurbished were said to have provided conditions that were clean and decent. But the number of assaults in the prison was said to be high. However, there had been no escapes since the last inspection.

But Dr McLellan was not finished with slopping out – he reported, 'Overall, levels of overcrowding, movements of prisoners in and out of the prison, and the issue of drugs make the day to day running of the prison difficult and can lead to a reduction in regime. The practice of "slopping out" has been repeatedly condemned in Inspectorate reports; yet it still exists in two Halls in Barlinnie. That could affect up to a maximum of 425 prisoners. The practice should be stopped.'

Incidentally Scotland's prisons are subject to regular inspection. A full inspection normally takes place every three years and examines all aspects of the establishment. Follow-up inspections are carried out in years where a full inspection does not take place and these examine points of note raised in previous inspections, significant changes since then, and explore issues arising from the establishment's own self-assessment.

The slopping out story, however, really began to grip popular interest when Glasgow's legions of avid newspaper readers were informed over their cornflakes that the previously mentioned Robert Napier, in the Bar-L on remand in 2001, had raised a legal challenge to being made to slop out under the European Convention of Human Rights. 'So what?' some of the hard-nosed readers might have thought, but even if they weren't in sympathy with the plight of jailbirds on humanitarian grounds, some readers were no doubt incensed on the fiscal front – Napier wanted five grand from the taxpayer. At the time of his claim he was in Barlinnie after failing to appear at the High Court on robbery, assault and abduction charges.

He said he found the conditions in the jail's C-Hall depressing and disgusting and they had resulted in a diminishment of his human dignity. He also said he suffered from eczema and that the slopping out had aggravated this medical condition. And in April 2004, three years after the initial complaint, Lord Bonomy, in a 100-page ruling, awarded him nearly half what he had claimed – £2,400. The noble lord found that slopping out violated articles three and eight of the European convention and the common law 'duty of care'. On the violation of article three he said: 'I am entirely satisfied that the petitioner was exposed to conditions of detention which taken together, were such as to damage his human rights, his human dignity and to arise in him feelings of anxiety, anguish, inferiority and humiliation.' Lord Bonomy could not have been clearer.

At this time the prison service was in the expensive process of phasing out the practice. Massive sums were involved – you do not simply wave a wand overnight and put toilets and wash hand basins in the hundreds of cells designed by the Victorians and built in solid blocks of stone. Providing basic facilities was enormously expensive and difficult. But it had to be done. At the time of the Napier judgement the Scottish National Party declared the decision of Lord Bonomy to be 'inevitable' and aimed to score a few political points by saying the Executive had been dragging its feet by not doing enough to end the practice earlier. Their then Justice Spokesperson Nicola Sturgeon said: 'This case was only ever going to go one way and now the Executive face hundreds of claims for compensation from other prisoners. Because of a failure to invest in prison conditions, they now face having to make compensation payments to convicted prisoners. A public figure with some experience of jails, as a political protester, Tommy Sheridan, then of the Scottish Socialist Party, called for an immediate end to slopping out. In jail for failing to pay Poll Tax, he said he had experienced the utter humiliation of the practice.

The long-awaited headline, 'Slopping out ends at Barlinnie' finally arrived on a million or so breakfast tables in August 2004, years after the 'humiliation' of Robert Napier. But the practice did continue for some months in other jails: Polmont, Perth, Saughton and Peterhead. However, Tony Cameron for the Prison Service said he was delighted that slopping out in Barlinnie had ended 122 years after its first block opened. 'This achievement has been made possible by the record level of investment in the Scottish Prison Service by the Scottish Executive supplemented by savings which SPS has made by becoming more efficient.' He added that, at the time in 2004, the total capital investment by SPS in the prison estate was running at almost £2m a week.

For the Scottish government, the then Justice Minister Cathy Jamieson said the ending of slopping out in the Bar-L was an important one for the prison service: 'This Executive is committed to improving the conditions in the prison estate we inherited.' She went on to point out that there had been sustained investment and that steps were being taken to accelerate reforms to improve conditions and make better use of custody. Aware of the public antipathy to anything that looked like going soft on crime, she made a pre-emptive strike: 'This is not about making life softer for offenders. Investment in fair prison conditions will also contribute to improved public safety. It's about giving experienced, professional prison staff the environment they need to effectively tackle the offending behaviour that brings too many repeat offenders back into jail time and time again.'

The decisions on how we run our jails and deal with lawbreakers are much influenced by politicians and they almost never agree on anything. So no surprise then that when Annabel Goldie for the Tories did acknowledge that she was glad slopping out was history she also added a few warning notes. She worried about 'floodgates' of potential claims opening in other prisons where the archaic practice still went on. She said: 'Sadly a life of crime sometimes does pay under this government. If they are not letting you out of jail early under the ludicrous automatic early release scheme, they are letting you escape from court, and now they might pay you for slopping out.' That's politics.

Fears about the knock-on effect of the Napier decision were well founded. In the spring of 2009 the financial cost was still rising. Where it will end is anyone's guess. There was a spell when it looked as if the problem could be contained. As the cons queued to make claims, the Executive tried to cut its losses believing that it was protected, to some extent at least, by a one-year time bar on claims under the European Convention of Human Rights. With the papers full of stories on what was becoming a bit of a farce, albeit one that angered the taxpayer, the politicians tried to cut their losses and a settlement was reached with 190 prisoners, which cost less than half a million pounds – chicken feed compared with the fears that the cost would run into millions.

But there was a shock to come in 2007 when the highest appeal court in the UK decided that the one-year time bar was not a runner in this case, raising the possibility that Scottish ministers could be sued for human rights breaches that occurred any time from 1999 onwards. It appears that though the Human Rights Convention had the one-year limit, nonetheless there is no time bar for cases brought under the Scotland Act and the Law Lords, in a 3-2 ruling, said the latter legislation should prevail. This ruling on a particular case was based not on slopping out directly, but on four men kept in segregation in prison – Andrew Somerville, Ricardo Blanco, Sammy Ralston – a man with a major place in Barlinnie history – and David Henderson. These men had claimed their human rights had been abused when they were forced to live in segregated conditions without recourse to representation. The overruling of the original 2006 belief that they were time barred seems to have changed the rules more than somewhat. Their case could now go ahead.

At the time of writing, figures released showed that 3,737 slopping out claims had been settled at a cost of more than

£11m and more than a thousand were currently being dealt with. Justice Minister Kenny MacAskill was frustrated and angry over Westminster's lack of action to close what some thought was a legal loophole on the matter of slopping out compensation. The whole business was becoming a nasty soap opera. What a mess on mess. And it could have been avoided if slopping out had been abolished many many years ago, as it would have been in a truly civilised society.

Also back in 2007 came a graphic report of an inspection by the authorities on the current state of affairs in the Bar-L. Barlinnie, it pointed out, is the largest prison in Scotland. The prisoners living there account for 20% of the total population in the system. One hall in Barlinnie can hold more prisoners than many other prisons. The report then moved on to the overcrowding situation, saying the prison has a design capacity of 1,018. In the period 1 April 2006 to 28 July 2006 the average daily population was 1,456: 43% above the design capacity. The Scottish Prison Service now contracts prisons to take a specified number of prisoners and for Barlinnie the figure is up to 1,222 prisoners. On top of this there are an agreed additional 417 prisoner places: a total of 1,639. But the design capacity remains at 1,018! And all this more than 100 years after the place was built.

The 2007 report stated bluntly: 'The damage caused by overcrowding and high prisoner numbers has been well documented in previous Inspectorate reports. Barlinnie has tried to manage these problems, but there is no obvious respite in the short-term. Over and above the sheer volume of prisoners, two other points are worth mentioning. Barlinnie has a complex population of various sentence types including 450–500 prisoners on remand at any one time. It also has to cope with an extremely 'needy' population of prisoners; many of the prisoners have a combination of addiction, behavioural and physical and mental health problems. The prison is currently coping with these issues.' That may be true, but the conditions are still horrendous. Ironically, the ending of slopping out has added to the problem in some aspects.

In A-Hall for example the report said there are 187 cells on four floors. '261 prisoners were living in 181 of these cells at the time of inspection. The floor space in each cell has been reduced because they have all been fitted with a toilet inside a cubicle. There is also a sink in each cell as well as a power point, television and kettle.

The reference to the television is interesting. The papers recently were getting themselves and their readers into a froth of anger about the 'luxury' of flat-screen TVs for prisoners. Is there any other kind now? And in any case the screens are small. Luxury is not a word to be used lightly in the context of Barlinnie.

The refurbishment of A-Hall was completed in 2004 and the reopening signalled the end of slopping out in Barlinnie. A prison service report at the time said: 'Many of the cells are very cramped with two prisoners living in them. A formal system of cell allocation should be introduced which identifies an acceptable amount of space for a prisoner to live in.

'Windows in the cells are high and do not let in much natural light. They are grilled over and have broad slats on the outside. Whilst this has the benefit of stopping prisoners throwing litter out of the windows and making the exercise yard untidy, it also restricts the amount of natural light and fresh air that can get into a cell. The general standard of decoration in the cells is acceptable. Indeed the communal areas are much brighter than they were during the previous full inspection in 2003. This makes the hall a much lighter, less oppressive environment.

There is very little space for interviewing available in the hall. A few cells have been converted into interview rooms but getting access to them can be difficult because the demand from specialist staff is great. This should be addressed.'

This fairly recent report is a down to earth, realistic picture of life in the jail, a life nothing like as cushy as outsiders tend to think. 'New showers and ablutions were fitted in the old slopping out areas during refurbishment. There are an adequate number of showers for the population and, two years after coming into use, they are still maintained to an excellent standard. Outside exercise is taken in a large yard adjacent to the hall. All prisoners can exercise in the yard at the same time. The yard is spacious and clean. The recreation room consists of snooker, pool, table tennis and a television. There are also four telephones, two of which do not have canopies. The room is a converted workshop and whilst it is quite bleak it is clean and functional.'

The week after the inspection, A-Hall introduced a servery system for meal times. This is a significant event, moving as it does away from the old plastic trays. Inspectors returned to see how the new system worked. The report said that, 'The improvements in the quality and presentation of the food were obvious. Prisoners commented very favourably on the new system. A rotating system is in place to allow all prisoners a fair chance at selecting their first choice. It is intended to introduce an advance choice menu system in the near future. This will bring A-Hall into line with most of the rest of the prison.

'There is no opportunity for communal eating in the hall. Prisoners collect their meals and return to their cell to eat. Cells are locked while they eat. The cramped nature of many of the cells means that many prisoners eat their meals sitting on their bed with their plates on their laps.'

The inspectors then turned their attention to B-Hall and again the overcrowding was highlighted. 'This hall holds convicted prisoners in 191 cells on four floors. Two hundred and seventy prisoners were living in 181 of these cells at the time of inspection. Many of the cells were said to be very cramped with two prisoners living there.' Another complaint was that the general standard of decoration in the hall is poor. 'The hall does not have a painting and decorating work party, which might help to improve standards.' It was pointed out that other prisons have used prisoners to resolve this problem, 'most successfully in Aberdeen where they have redecorated the entire accommodation area.'

The B-Hall recreation area at the time of this inspection was the Activities Centre in the industrial complex. 'The room is a converted workshop and is adjacent to a well-stocked library with an extensive range of books, magazines, periodicals and computer games.' B-Hall was ahead of A-Hall in the business of serving food as it had now introduced a servery system for meals. 'This is a major improvement. Prisoners commented very favourably on the new system. An advance choice menu system is also now well established and works well. Again there was no communal eating, a civilizing influence, and prisoners collected their food and returned to their cells to eat. The doors were locked while they were doing so.' Officers in B-Hall said that because there wasn't enough time at the weekend to collect the plates and cutlery from prisoners to be washed in the hall dishwasher, they used paper plates instead. 'Prisoners do not get the opportunity to get rid of the dirty paper plates before being locked up.'

The story of C-Hall, the main remand hall, painted a similar picture though the records showed that there could be a hundred movements a day in this hall: 50 in, 50 out. Again there was overcrowding.

D-Hall was slightly different in that it has four separate sections, all of which have access to in-cell sanitation. All prisoners have access to time in the fresh air and to inside recreation, as well as the opportunity to visit the Activity Centre. 'Each section has a minimum of two telephones. All meals are served from the new servery trolleys: food was hot and well presented.' Included in the four sections is 'the Residential Care Unit, which has 42 cells. On the day of inspection there were 43 prisoners living there. These are usually short-term prisoners who have mental health issues or require some form of support. There is one disabled cell, which was occupied. There is a link with the Health Centre and prisoners can self-refer. The Unit is occasionally used as a 'stepping stone' back into the mainstream system. The facility itself is maintained to a good standard of decoration and cleanliness and relationships between staff and prisoners are good. However, prisoners within this regime spend a significant part of their day locked up in their cells due to a lack of opportunity to participate in any work or structured activity.'

Anyone sent to jail for a sexual offence can be in constant danger from other inmates: hardened criminals who would kill your granny, as they say in Glasgow, are remarkably, consistently, and sometimes violently unforgiving of such offenders. In D-Hall the Sex Offender Unit had 44 cells and on the day of inspection 65 prisoners were living there. 'There was a good atmosphere within the area and both staff and prisoners reported positive relationships. On the day of inspection there were a large number of prisoners locked in cells, despite the fact that education was on offer.' The other two sections in D-Hall contain a range of prisoners serving different lengths of sentence and the report concluded, 'Overall, although prisoners and staff were generally content with facilities and regime in D-Hall there is little to do and prisoners spend much of their time locked within their cells. This was due to lack of work opportunities and structured activities being available. This should be addressed.'

Finally to E-Hall, which fulfils two very important functions for Barlinnie. It houses the First Night Centre on the top floor and the other three floors house most of the prisoners on protection. The First Night Centre is a specialized area that performs a vital service. The shock to the system that a first night in a jail like Barlinnie produces cannot be underestimated, especially for someone like a white collar criminal who has no experience of doing time and is not a member of a family or a community, like too many in Glasgow, where the clang of cell doors behind you is regarded as an inevitable rite of passage. To be stripped, searched, your belongings removed, scrubbed clean and given prison clothes and dowsed with the grim reality that you have completely lost your freedom and entered a nightmare world inhabited by a curious mixture of old lags, young tearaways, morose loners, dangerous characters and the very occasional enthusiastic self-educator is an experience that can induce deep depression and mental ill health in even the strongest of personalities. A humane approach here by the staff and the understanding that it can take months, perhaps years, for a prisoner to come to terms with his fate is important. And Barlinnie has made giant steps in this respect.

Most of the report's observations also apply generally to E-Hall. Food takes on an unnatural importance when you are imprisoned. It is not five-star fodder. In E-Hall prisoners have a pre-selection choice menu system (except those in the First

Night Centre). According to the report everyone is served his meal from a servery.

Letham Hall is a prefabricated building which acts as the local 'top-end' hall for Barlinnie, a home for the good guys, the non troublemakers who have, over the years, accepted and adapted to the prison regime. Letham houses convicted prisoners who have been assessed as suitable having been through A-Hall, B-Hall, D-Hall or E-Hall. It does not hold any prisoners on protection. There are no special cells.

The day the report was made there were 64 out of 76 cells in use in five sections on two floors, three upstairs and two downstairs. 'Only one section in the hall has single occupancy, although all of the cells are the same size. The prisoners in the single cells are designated to these cells because they work in certain work parties that require some shift working. Many of the cells are very cramped with two prisoners living there. Prisoners have a key to their own door and can access night sanitation and shower facilities during lock up periods. The hall is segmented into the five sections for control purposes by the use of grille gates during these periods. There is CCTV coverage in all communal areas. Windows in the cells in Letham Hall are large and not blocked in any way and therefore let in a lot of natural light. The general standard of decoration in the cells is good. However, interview space is limited although most of the prisoners are out at work most of the day so a quiet area can usually be found. There is a shower and ablutions area in each section. Whilst there is an adequate number of showers some were in need of repair or replacement.'

These 'top end' cons in Letham have a pre-selection choice menu system but again the food was taken away to be eaten in a cell. On Letham the report concluded, in rather humane manner that, 'Given its status as the local "top end", the opportunity to dine in association should be offered.' I like the use of the word dining in this context, but no matter how it has improved over the years it is not fine dining as defined by the celebrity chefs. But it is not 'chew and spew', as the Australians say, either. In the old days the menu was chalked on to a blackboard – now prisoners get a paper menu with multiple choices.

One of the blackboard menus of the 1980s I came across was typical:

Breakfast
Porridge [naturally!] and milk.
Grilled sausage
Tea, bread and marg

Dinner
Liver and onions
Or mince pie
Or fried chicken
Potatoes or chips, veg
Semolina

Tea
Cheese and onion flan, baked beans
Tea, bread, marg, jam

Supper
Half pint tea, fruit scone.

This contrasts with what is described as 'Ordinary Summer Menu 2009', the latest on offer. Each prisoner gets a sheet with multiple choices; the meals mentioned here are from the 'blue menu' for week three in the month. The inmates are urged to fill in their name, prison number, and cell location in the appropriate boxes. They are given a warning that any menus unmarked or covered in graffiti will result in the miscreant arbitrarily being given choice No. 3. Here is the menu for one Thursday.

Breakfast [shock horror, no porridge]
Beverage pack – morning roll, sunflower spread, 250ml One Milk, bran flakes, preserve portion.

Lunch [now changed from the more down-market '80s term 'dinner']
Three choices of main course:
Chicken and mushroom pie, potatoes and peas, OR
Turkey salad sandwich pack, OR
Fried rice and Chinese curry sauce.
[The final choice has an indication beside it that it is suitable for fish-eating vegetarians and the explanation that fish-free vegetarians will be offered an alternative when fish is the vegetarian choice.]
Portion of fresh fruit

Tea
Soup of the Day,
Three choices of main course :
Sweet and sour pork and boiled rice, OR
Gammon steak, potatoes and diced carrot, OR
Two rolls and cheese portion.
Pineapple slices and custard.

On paper it sounds good enough, but in institutional surroundings the food is in reality pretty basic. But suitable meals for inmates, often bored out of their mind and with horrific diets when out on the streets, is important. At least there are not regular helpings of a Glasgow salad – a plate of chips. Reasonable meals are vital in keeping prisoners in health, the place calm and in helping good relationships with the officers. The little poem/song from many years ago, mentioned elsewhere in the book, 'The Barlinnie Hotel', made reference to the fact that jailbirds didn't lay eggs in the Bar-L. But times change and now there is the treat of a boiled egg on Saturdays and Sundays. But in the week's menus quoted there was no porridge. Maybe now we need a new cliché – doing cereal.

Printed menus for every prisoner, yes. But there is no sign of a wine list. But that doesn't mean the Bar-L is a totally dry area. In every prison in the world it is the ultimate challenge – apart from escaping! – for the inmates to make some secret hooch. After all, booze is a major factor in how many of the denizens of the Bar-L ended up there. In the booze-fuelled crime stakes there is every chance that Glaswegians would come out as world champions. And the ingenuity that goes into smuggling chemical stimulants into the prison is also channeled into making hooch from the ingredients found inside the prison. Pizza bases and bread generally can have the last traces of yeast squeezed out of them and with stolen sugar, and other ingredients nicked from the kitchens, some simulation of an alcoholic beverage can be produced. It might not get into the good wine or whisky guide but prison hooch can satisfy one important drinking criterion – it can get you out of your mind.

Down the years there have been various attempts at illicit breweries in the prison, but the daddy of them all came in October 2008 when 25 litres of potent homemade hooch was discovered in Scotland's biggest prison. The vile tasting stuff – made from oranges, ketchup, bread, sugar and water – was uncovered in the aforementioned Letham Hall, home to the trusties. It was a huge haul. A prison source told the *Sun*: 'Some of the cons who make it have become real experts – they think they are Steve McQueen and James Garner producing their moonshine behind closed doors.' But he added the obvious caveat that the more you make the harder it is to hide it. And the drunker the cons get the more obvious it is what is going on. You could say success breeds failure in this specialist area.

Considering the links between Barlinnie and booze it is no real surprise, just good marketing, that at one stage you could pop into the Drovers pub in Gallowgate and have a wee swallow of what was called Barlinnie Bevvy, a nice little whisky with pride of place on the gantry of this legendary pub. The locals took to it like ducks to water, after all it was drink, but when news of this unusual label filtered down the road to the prison itself it was not well received. Indeed, according to the word on the streets, a rather terse letter was sent from HMP Barlinnie, Lee Avenue, Riddrie to the Drovers. But it seems any rough waters whipped up by the sale of Barlinnie Bevvy were swiftly smoothed with the delivery to the then prison staff of a package that was alleged to have given off a loud clink of glass when moved. If only all the Bar-L worries would go away so easily.

7

FAMOUS FACES
AND DIRTY UNDERWEAR

What do you expect when one of the most famous men in the
world turns up as a visitor? Huge crowds, of course, and that's
what happened when Nelson Mandela travelled from South
Africa to meet Abdelbaset Ali Mohmed al-Megrahi, the Libyan
man convicted of the Lockerbie bombing, on a diplomatic excur-
sion to see for himself, in June 2002, how the alleged mass
murderer was being treated. Nelson Mandela also discussed a
campaign for the Libyan to serve his sentence in a prison in
his own country. Everyone, but everyone, who has met Mandela
speaks of his kindness, gentleness and good manners. Even on
a commercial flight when people cannot resist breaking into
his privacy, he has time to chat and take a genuine interest in
his fellow passengers. A little vignette from his Barlinnie visit
underlines the humanity of this remarkable historic figure, a
man who himself had spent long years in jail on Robben Island.
Most of the crowd hoping to meet him at the prison were posi-
tioned around the reception and the main gates.

Everyone on the staff wanted a glimpse of the great man.
The wellwishers were rows deep. But as he passed through the
throng, Mandela stopped for a moment to survey the scene.
He looked to the edge of the crowd and spotted a young prison

officer right at the back. He said, 'You, sir, step down here,' and when the surprised young officer made his way to the front Mandela shook his hand warmly, giving him a moment he would never forget. Humbly, Nelson Mandela remarked that he, too, knew what it was like to be in the back row and not really noticed. Incidentally the use of the word 'sir' is something of a Mandela trademark – he uses it all the time. Maybe it's a hangover from his own jail time. The great leader then went into the jail to meet al-Megrahi, who was still declaiming his innocence, and to inspect his quarters. But he politely declined an offer by the Governor to show him the cellblocks as distinct from Gaddafi's Café, as the area where al-Megrahi was held was nicknamed in the press. Nelson Mandela had seen enough tiny jail cells to last him a lifetime!

The nickname of the quarters which held al-Megrahi doesn't seem far off the mark. There is real reluctance in official quarters to confirm or deny conditions in the 'café'. Since al-Megrahi was convicted at a special court held under Scottish law at Camp Zeist in the Netherlands of killing 259 passengers and crew on Pan Am flight 103 and 11 residents of Lockerbie in 1988 the case has been a diplomatic minefield with Britain and Libya and the United States often in conflict and continually changing stances. The case was even important enough to bring UN general secretary Kofi Annan to Glasgow on a trip out east to the prison. No wonder officialdom gives a body swerve commenting on the conditions Megrahi was held in in Barlinnie. But you can't just brush away the Scottish Press. And towards the end of 2003 the *News of the World* reporters, digging around to prove or disprove the street talk about the café, struck newspaper gold. The Libyan described by the red top as a 51-year-old monster was shown in pictures to be luxuriating in a suite with a kitchen and sitting room and a bedroom with ensuite toilet. At this time, it should be noted, some in the Bar-L were still slopping out.

The photographs, said to be smuggled out by a prisoner outraged at the treatment of a mass killer, also showed floral curtains. Some of the officers guarding him must have thought they were back in the good old days of the Special Unit! The ex-con told the now defunct *News of the World* that: 'I can understand why he has to be kept in solitary for his own safety, but does he have to have luxuries as well?' The outrage was felt worldwide and Americans who had lost relatives in the bombing were outspoken in their condemnation of what was going on. No matter how much official head shaking and dodging of the question went on, the newspaper view of the cushy life of the convicted bomber inside seems fairly accurate. It may not have been the Ritz, as some said, but it was no tiny cell shared with a chib-marked Glasgow con and a couple of piss pots.

When the alleged Libyan ex-intelligence officer showed up at the prison, feelings were running high. The prisoners were said to have 'howled with hatred' in the echoing halls as the helicopter bringing him from the trial in the Netherlands noisily swooped down to land. And that comment from a con who understood the threats to his safety from other prisoners was right on the mark. It was freely said that some prisoners would like to kill such a high-profile inmate for the notoriety it would bring. And there were few higher profile criminals around than the so-called Lockerbie Bomber. Others might have sought to simply avenge the Pan Am bombing. But al-Megrahi survived. Indeed, later in his sentence there were even reports of him playing in football kickarounds with his fellow inmates.

Eventually he was moved out of Barlinnie to Greenock where there was less newspaper talk about his conditions. All along there have been those who believe in his innocence, including many in high places, and in mid 2009 he was mired in yet another appeal amid more pleas to have him sent home. He was suffering from what was said to be terminal prostate cancer.

One of the many difficult tasks of any governor is dealing with the steady stream of complaints, some from the prison equivalent of barrack room lawyers, some just trying to ease the slow passing of prison time by starting long drawn-out disputes that, at least, put some vague meaning into an aimless life. Nothing like a sense of victimisation to keep your brain cells active. All governors are well used to the letters of complaint from their charges. The letters, too, when the prisoner is literate enough, tend to be long. There are no deadlines for prison scribblers. And their letters are usually predictable and mostly somewhat less than eloquent. But, as in every walk of life, there are exceptions. A good example is the intelligent and considered missive from prisoner 133977 (cell 34, A Block) in the spring of 2001 to the then Governor, Roger Houchin.

Prisoner 133977 was no run-of-the-mill Glasgow villain; he was a man cast from a different mould from his fellow prisoners. Brian Quail was a nuclear peace protestor, an intelligent, literate and active campaigner against nuclear weapons, particularly those held in the Navy base at Faslane on the Clyde, not far from Barlinnie. No doubt that the Russians at the height of the cold war had this base targeted for its nukes and no doubt, too, that Barlinnie and Glasgow generally were in danger of being vaporised in such a strike. The controversy that has swirled round Barlinnie in its almost 130 years of life would have become academic! Brian Quail was in the Bar-L because of his conscience and his concern for humanity, though the actual crime he had committed to get himself cast into the 'big house' in Glasgow's east end was the simple matter of the non-payment of a fine of a few quid imposed on him for protesting offences, breach of the peace, etc. There could be no questioning Brain Quail's sincerity.

In his letter he told Roger Houchin that: 'I wish to make a number of observations which may provide you with a better understanding of the situation from a prisoner's perspective, and hopefully thereby help you to achieve a better ordering of the prison. You must be conscious of the fact that many inmates are unwilling to express their opinions through lack of confidence, feelings of inadequacy in writing skills, or apprehension about the possible outcome of any such efforts. I feel therefore that I am writing not only on my own behalf, but also in the interests of many others in prison.' He also remarked that he would no doubt return to Barlinnie in the future and asked to be allowed to explain the thinking behind his refusal to pay what he called the 'paltry' fine of £30.

He pointed out that he was a member of Trident Ploughshares, a group pledged to take peaceful non-violent direct action against the deployment of Trident by the British state. No doubt aware that this letter would reach the public he took the opportunity to point out that each Trident nuclear sub had a large number of nuclear bombs, each more than eight times more powerful than the bomb dropped on Hiroshima. After some more powerful words justifying the background to his incarceration, he turned to the points he wanted to raise on his spell in Barlinnie.

'At my reception I explained to the medical staff that I had a double coronary by-pass, that I was prone to trachyitis and bronchitis, and for these reasons felt entitled to insist on a non-smoking environment in my cell. This was noted on my medical form, and I was told to inform the hall officer of these facts. This I did, but my request was brusquely dismissed as being impossible. I consequently spent 23 hours a day with a cellmate who smoked constantly, even waking up several times a night to do so. I feel that this was a direct assault on my health and I am convinced that it contravened my basic human rights as defined in European Union law. In the circumstances I took no further action, but determined that in the future I would seek legal address were I subjected to similar abuse again.'

He then moved on to the contentious subject of slopping out. In his view, and that of many others, even back in 2001, the fact that such an 'obnoxious' practice was still in use in the twenty-first century was almost unbelievable. He invited Roger Houchin, if he had any doubts, to join him and experience slopping out for himself.

That invitation was easy to decline and it also has to be pointed out that the request was naive. Many prison officers were as disgusted by the process of slopping out as the prisoners. And the officers suffered, too. Today in Barlinnie you can still see the shafts where the excrement was sloshed down from the upper flats to the ground floor, under supervision of the officers. No surprise then the old joke: How do you recognise a prison officer? – He is the guy who can go at least three minutes without breathing!

Other aspects of the Quail Letter were less dramatic, but still demonstrated a basic lack of humanity, a recognition that while many of the prison population had reading and writing difficulties and merited schooling rather than the services of a library, for certain prisoners to be denied access to newspapers was a severe punishment. There were other little niggles like the fact what when Brian Quail's partner tried to arrange a visit, no one answered when she phoned. Mind you, that is a complaint that can on occasion be made of any large organisation.

He went on to mention what he called a relatively minor point, though many would put it much higher than that on any scale of complaints. He said: 'When I was issued with prison uniform I was given jeans and a shirt of suitable size. The underwear however seemed to have been issued on a "one size for all" basis. I am 63 years of age and considerably larger than the young men who were my fellow convicts. I spent my time waddling around with my underpants below my crotch, stretched between each leg of my trousers. They were about half the size needed to circumvent my regrettably large waist. Likewise my vest was halfway up my chest all the time. Not very comfortable.'

Brian Quail was not the last to raise the issue of underpants in the Bar-L. It surfaced again in 2007 when inmates complained of being forced to wear dirty and ill-fitting underwear. Then as always the prison was overcrowded and it was the only jail in Scotland to ban prisoners wearing their own clothing. The cons complained that they were given prison issue underpants, socks, and vests which could be stained or not the right size. The Chief Inspector, Dr Andrew McLellan, said the issue was of concern. 'You have to take what you are given. The underwear might fit or it might not, it might be unstained or not. I think it is a very important thing if you don't get the chance to wear your own underwear. We have seen underwear which has been washed but I would not call it clean.' He recommended personal underwear to be issued to individual inmates and suggested that prisoners were also allowed to wear their own clothes on family visits.

Brian Quail's letter to the governor was not an entirely negative letter. There was praise for the officers, a group that even the Scottish Prison Service itself admits does not have a particularly high image. 'In spite of popular rumour and my own apprehensions, the guards were relaxed and unaggressive – some indeed were downright friendly. One officer took pity on my obvious withdrawal pains and took the trouble to acquire a book for me – for which I was and am very grateful.'

The letter ended with some pertinent and helpful, and well meaning, observations though there was a touch of what a prison service pro might regard as 'teaching your granny to suck eggs':

'I appreciate that yours is a uniquely difficult profession because you are dealing with people who, without exception, do not wish to be under your authority. No one wants to be in prison. Resentment and anger are potentially ever-present dangers. All over the prison I saw notices affirming a "no violence" policy. Perhaps if some of the repressive and destructive aspects of the penal system were addressed, there might be less chance of a build-up of repressed anger. Slopping out and the sheer maddening boredom of isolation in a cell are themselves sources of resentment and violence. I am sure you appreciate the cogency of these observations through your own years of experience in the prison service. Yours sincerely, Brian Quail.'

Brian Quail's reference to a possible return to Barlinnie as part of his ongoing nuclear arms protests was not wide of the mark. Later that year he found himself in the dock, in Edinburgh this time, and jail beckoned yet again. But it was to be a different jail this time, Edinburgh's Saughton. He was leaving the dock in Edinburgh Sheriff Court having confirmed his plea, on yet another charge related to the Faslane protests, and was looking forward to a couple of hours sightseeing in the capital. (The trial would be completed later.) It was not to be. The law had this peacenik in its sights and his way was blocked by two police officers who produced a warrant for his arrest for another unpaid fine. So it was off to a night in St Leonard's police station then a week in Saughton jail in Edinburgh, not Barlinnie.

Quail points out that this switch of prison was odd; maybe something to do with that letter to Governor Houchin. In Saughton, Quail was given a cell to himself. He comments: 'The atmosphere in general was a lot more relaxed than the infamous Bar-L. I was allowed to keep my watch, trainers, socks and underwear. There was a little library on the first floor where my cell was.

'The ubiquitous drug culture was a sad evidence of so many young lives blighted; the undercurrent of violence a familiar sensation, though I never felt personally threatened. (Being three times the age of most of the inmates I dare say I was not seen as a threat!) I fasted for the six days of my stay, a private and silent act of spiritual solidarity with those who starve perforce while we squander billions on the killing industry.'

Brian Quail made many headlines in his campaigning against nuclear weapons, but perhaps much of it passed over the heads of his fellow inmates, most of the time. But other 'headliners' were a different story. It is a fair bet that following football and boxing, when they can, is a major interest of Barlinnie inmates. And sometimes the prisoners get closer to the stars than some of the paying fans in stadiums or sporting clubs. It is also a fair bet that at any given time the five great cell blocks of the jail hold a goodly proportion of 'blue noses', i.e. fans of the Rangers Football Club. So it is easy to imagine the excitement in 1994 when one of the Rangers first team, Duncan Ferguson, found himself in Barlinnie. Ferguson had been involved in what was described as an off-the-ball assault on John McStay of Raith Rovers, one of Kirkcaldy's finest. The incident was so violent that the police took an interest in what took place on the field and was seen by many thousands in the stadium and perhaps millions on TV. The intervention of the law was a rare event at a major soccer match.

Ferguson seems to have taken his punishment like a man and went on to have a successful career with Everton, who bought him for £4m, a stratospheric sum no doubt to his fellow inmates. A strong-willed man, he kept his rough house tendencies mostly under control in his subsequent career and went on to earn a medal for Everton against Manchester United in the 1995 FA Cup Final, a game the Liverpool side won 1-0. But he was always a bit of a controversialist and in season 1997–98 he unilaterally decided to end his career as a Scotland player even though some football pundits thought he was at the height of his powers. His connection with Barlinnie added a curious little twist to the prison story: his jail time inspired a piece of classical music called 'Barlinnie Nine'. This epic was composed by Osmo Tapio Räihälä and the 'nine' in the title came from the number on Ferguson's Rangers shirt.

Räihälä said: 'I got the idea for the composition when Duncan Ferguson was facing jail and had just become something of a cult figure for Everton. It takes into account the contradictions in him: he has an aggressive side but there is a lyrical undertone to him.' The gentler and generous side of the footballer's nature is also underlined by his time at Everton when he was a regular visitor to sick children at Alder Hey Children's Hospital. He was a hugely popular figure at this hospital. He did not confine his good works for charity to Alder Hey and often took gifts with him on visits to seriously ill children in their own homes.

'Barlinnie Nine' was premiered on 20 April 2005 by a Finnish Radio orchestra, conducted by Sakari Oramo, in the Finlandia Hall, Helsinki. Serendipitously, at the time Ferguson was helping set up a league win for the 'Toffees' against the legendary Reds for the first time in ten years. This all produced a remarkable quote from the composer of 'Barlinnie Nine'. Räihälä said: 'There

COURTESY OF HEATHERBANK MUSEUM OF SOCIAL WORK

It is difficult to visualise the true size of the forbidding building that is Barlinnie from the main gate at Lee Avenue, Riddrie. This stark shot captures the fearsome image of the prison, and its immense size. Behind these huge dark stone walls ten killers ended their life in the infamous Hanging Shed.

©HERALD AND TIMES GROUP

e Hanging Sh

A telephone call 35 years ago began a trail of events which left an indelible mark on one of Scotland's top lawyers. In an extract from his forthcoming book he relives the death of a teenager – despite appeals and petitions

eping juror, a tee

The last man to go to the gallows was Tony Miller in December 1960. Aged 19, Miller's conviction for his part in the murder of an elderly gay man caused huge controversy and thousands signed a petition to save the life of the teenager. The law took its grim course regardless.

CROWN COPYRIGHT NATIONAL ARCHIVES OF SCOTLAND

But if Miller had much public sympathy, the same cannot be said of serial killer Peter Manuel who, knowing the game was finally up, is reputed to have run the last few steps to the gallows and the drop into eternity on July 11, 1958.

©MIRRORPIX.COM

The height of the perimeter wall is emphasised when you look at the massive structure of a cell block.

©HERALD AND TIMES GROUP

©HERALD AND TIMES GROUP

There was little to smile about inside, but on the day of sentence in court a real Glasgow hard man has to have a grin on his face when sent down. Here Walter Norval (top left), seems unperturbed at facing around a decade behind bars.

The prison van entering the old main gate was a familiar sight to Glaswegians as it roamed the city centre taking villains from the 'big hoose' in the east end to and from court.

Even in this mug shot Arthur Thompson Snr hints at an interest in smart dressing with a sweater that would look at home in a suburban golf club. The man nicknamed 'The Last Godfather' had a penchant for silk ties and snappy suits and would tell anyone who would listen that he was a 'retired businessman'. Some man, some business!

Porridge was naturally on the old menu, but these days there is a more enlightened policy with an occasional taste of exotic food and more fresh fruit. It is hardly Gordon Ramsay style though!

A lonely figure tries to escape the boredom of confinement with a book. The days of slopping out are thankfully gone, but the Bar-L cells are as constricting as ever and overcrowding means that for many cell sharing is still going on.

The most controversial experiment in Scotland's penal history was the Barlinnie Special Unit. It was devised to give Lifers hope, moderate their behaviour and tap any talent they had. It worked. But it was closed down in a swirl of controversy in the nineties.

©HERALD AND TIMES GROUP

©HERALD AND TIMES GROUP

©HERALD AND TIMES GROUP

It never was the palace its critics painted it as, but at least the walls and cells could be decorated. Hugh Collins and Jimmy Boyle were the two most publicised of many success stories, men reformed, their lives turned around in the BSU.

Down the years all sorts of events and concerts have been put on inside the walls, everything from jazz groups to choirs, experimental plays and theatre of all kinds. It is a vital part of the process of redemption and reform.

Currently the remarkable volunteer group Theatre Nemo is doing valuable work behind bars helping the prisoners to express themselves artistically. The results of the art classes go on show and are spectacular.

Stairway to controversy... convicted terrorist bomber Abdelbaset Ali al-Megrahi, released on compassionate grounds by the Scottish Government in August 2009, boards a jet at Prestwick en-route to Libya where he was met with a hero's welcome that caused anger world wide.

In Megrahi's time at Barlinnie he was visited by both Nelson Mandela and Kofi Annan, not the sort of world statesmen you normally meet in Riddrie. Mandela made many friends in Glasgow with his gracious attitude.

To be in the Bar-L did not disqualify you from appearing in the tabloids. Two of the regulars in the redtops were a young looking Paul Ferris and a wilder looking TC Campbell, the man wrongly convicted of the ice cream war fires.

Rioters on the chimney heads – perhaps the most famous image in Barlinnie's long history. In January 1987 accusations by prisoners of ill treatment resulted in a major riot with prison officers held hostage and part of the prison wrecked. It ended peacefully after five fraught days, the longest such siege in Scotland.

Bill McKinlay, Governor from 2001 to 2010, is a humane and outspoken leader who drove forward programmes to improve life for prisoners and staff. But it is his belief that the prison has served its time and needs to be replaced by a modern establishment.

The recently appointed deputy Rhona Hotchkiss was recruited from outside the prison service to serve at the highest level and to help introduce some new thinking on prison problems.

Chaplains are vital and one of the longest serving of the part-time breed is Eddie Simpson, a remarkable minister whose Kirk is in an affluent Southside suburb and who has served with humour, skill and compassion in the 'big hoose' for more than 20 years.

I was describing Duncan as a failure in Finland, and thousands of miles away at Everton he rises like a phoenix from the ashes to score against Manchester United. If there are gods of football up there, this proves they have got a most twisted sense of humour.' Duncan Ferguson now lives in the sunshine of Majorca, though I doubt if he is still a pigeon breeder, a hobby which was another indication of the gentler side of a complex man.

But, for sure, his circumstances are much different from those of another sporting hero who spent time languishing in Barlinnie – Scott Harrison. Harrison threw away a glittering boxing career that saw him win the WBO world featherweight title in 2002 and successfully defend it. Harrison, like many of his fellow inmates, could blame his problems on drugs, alcohol and depression. After his Bar-L episode he was sentenced to two and a half years in prison by a court in Spain and detained by Spain's national police on landing at Malaga in April 2009. In 2006 he had been in trouble with the Spanish authorities over an alleged car theft and assault. He was also declared bankrupt and stripped of his WBO title. His boxing licence was taken away for bringing the sport into disrepute. And in 2008 he was sent to Barlinnie for drink driving and other offences. The Spanish courts issued an international arrest after he failed to attend a court hearing – difficult to do as he was in Barlinnie at the time, serving four months of an eight-month sentence. It was a sad downfall reminiscent of the booze-fuelled descent into tragedy of Benny Lynch.

Farcical rather than tragic would be the adjective of choice for the story of one of the most remarkable men to taste porridge in Barlinnie – Stephen Gough, aka The Naked Rambler. This crusader for nudity and self-determination walked the length of Britain from Land's End to John O'Groats, wearing only his boots and a rucksack, in 2003. He was repeatedly arrested on various charges but did achieve his aim of completing the walk. In June 2005 he started a repeat journey. At first the complaints were even fewer than on the 2003/4 odyssey except when he reached Scotland. The differences between Scottish and English law caused this eccentric more trouble north of the border, since a breach of the peace charge was always a threat. He was in and out of jails all over the place, despite hardly being a serious danger to society. And he certainly added an intriguing little footnote to the story of Barlinnie's celebrity inhabitants with an interesting arrest. Leaving the jail, at the end of one sentence, he was held again a few metres from the front gate. PCs Amanda Daly and James Clark were waiting for him when he left the jail and he was detained after refusing to put on his clothes. But there was a twist this time. In Glasgow Sheriff court Sheriff Margaret Gimblett cleared him of breach of the peace after hearing his lawyer point out that for a breach to have occurred, members of the public would have to be placed in a state of fear and alarm and be disturbed or upset. This he said had not been proved since he was arrested so quickly. Sheriff Gimblett agreed. But his freedom was short lived and he was rearrested in the court's foyer and he was off to jail yet again!

Supporters of his fight for the right to live in nudity were outraged. One supporter commented that in England he walked from Land's End to the Scottish border with only two arrests followed by immediate release and that 'civilisation continued'. This spokesman argued that 'it seems generally accepted that he has not harmed anyone and that he is not a danger to anyone. Indeed there is strong evidence that it is prudery, not nudity, that is harmful. Despite that, in Scotland, his conduct is considered so heinous by some parts of the police and legal system that he is required to be jailed.'

In the first walk in 2005 he was also arrested for leaving Saughton with no clothes. He must have been one special Barlinnie prisoner. You wonder what the assorted knife men, thieves and druggies who were his companions in jail thought of his crusade.

8

BROKEN BATONS,
BROKEN HEADS

There are many players in the never-ending war on crime on the streets of Glasgow – the perpetrators of violence them-selves, the cops who track them down and jail them, the staff of the prisons who contain the bad guys when convicted and try to send them back outside after their term behind bars in a condition that makes them less threatening to society, well-paid lawyers by the hundred and many, many overworked and under-appreciated social workers. And day after day there are thousands of newspaper readers who avidly follow the goings on in what – regardless of recent massive improvements – can still be a violent and dangerous city for some of its residents. Keeping track of crime can be a life-long armchair hobby, equally fascinating whether followed from TV or radio or the pages of the red tops or the less sensational, but equally interested broadsheets. Glaswegians are world famous for their appetite for news. And crime is always on the menu.

Readers of the crime pages got some tasty reading on one of the most dramatic days in the history of Barlinnie, 21 December 1934. But the grim prison out in the east end of the city was not actually page-one news that day – the full story of a remarkable bloody weekend in the Bar-L took some time to emerge. But prisons were on Page One, with Peterhead for once outplaying Barlinnie on that day.

The *Record* reported the sad news that the famous actress Jessie Matthews had lost a baby not long after its birth. And RAF planes were searching the Syrian Desert for a missing Dutch airliner. But the lead in the paper was 'Chained convict sensation'. The chained convict was none other than that Scottish criminal legend Gentle Johnny Ramensky. Ramensky was no stranger to Barlinnie, prisons generally or lurid headlines. The son of Lithuanian immigrant parents, Johnny was born in the Lanarkshire mining village of Glenboig in 1906 and became perhaps the most skilled and most famous safebreaker in Britain. The exploits of this 'peterman', as the criminal fraternity called safebreakers, entertained and fascinated Glasgow newspaper readers for decades.

And he served his country well in time of war. He joined the commandos in 1943 and became an instructor in the art of safe blowing. Many times he was parachuted behind enemy lines to break safes and steal enemy documents. Ahead of the front line he broke into safes as the Eighth Army moved across North Africa, including a raid on the headquarters of Rommel himself. He also broke into the strong rooms and safes of Goering's headquarters in Schorfheide in Germany. But he could never stop the safe breaking habit even when out of the army and after the war he was back in his old routine.

In his career he managed to get himself sentences adding up to more than 50 years. And he was responsible for changes in the way prisons were run. To better understand the emotions behind the headlines of December 1934, and why he was page-one news, even before his army exploits, it is important to realise the position Ramensky held in the public consciousness. He was 'Gentle Johnny', a folk hero no less. His nickname came about because he seldom if ever resisted arrest. If the police felt his collar he went quietly to the cells to take his medicine. And it is interesting to note that he was often the victim of his own success. Detectives arriving at a crime scene and noting that it looked a sophisticated job shrugged their shoulders and said: 'Ramensky!' His gentle side showed remarkably when, after one arrest, he warned the authorities 'that care should be taken' opening a safe he had robbed. He did not want any amateur hurt by the gelignite he had left behind.

Back in 1934 he had been the only man ever to have escaped from Peterhead. So inside yet again for another safe he'd blasted open, he was sent to solitary and clapped in leg irons, in-humane treatment even in those days. The barbaric use of such cruel restraint on such a gentle character leaked to the public and caused outrage. This led the then Secretary of State to order a review of the prison service and leg irons was banned there-after.

As the Glasgow public devoured the stories flowing from Peterhead, trouble was breaking out on their doorstep in Barlinnie. And the seeds of the trouble all those years ago would touch a chord with anyone who read about another episode in the prison, many years later. There are similarities in what went on in the mid-thirties to what happened in the closing years of the century.

It is not really a surprise. Anyone with even the most fleeting experience of working at the coal face in the journalists' trade remembers some old hack or other who spent his time diluting the enthusiasm of fresh-faced young kids new to the news room, and bursting to make a name in the writing business, by exclaiming at every opportunity to anyone who would listen that there is nothing new under the sun. A favourite expres-sion of such wizened and cynical journos was that in news stories 'only the names change'. This is the stuff of cliché and caricature. But at the risk of falling into that trap, I have to say after too many years in the trade that there is something of a truth in such pontificating. The story of the Bar-L is no exception. In its long life it has seen riots and disturbances that could have come out of the script of a Hollywood movie written with James Cagney in mind. On the prisoners' side it seems rioting on the roof, planning an escape or smashing a cell is something of cyclical pattern – 'only the names change'! Likewise for those in the business of imprisoning the villains who roam the streets of Glasgow and at the same time trying to make them fit for society on their release. 'Pioneering' schemes to reform and rehabilitate the denizens of gangland are a regular recurring feature of the penal system.

In Glasgow today you will still get pub arguments about the success or failure of the Barlinnie Special Unit – aka the Wendy House or the Nutcracker Suite – which created worldwide interest from its inauguration in 1972 until it was closed down in 1994 amid lurid allegations of a lax regime that had an elite breed of super criminal luxuriating in drugs and sex behind bars. The Unit had massive press coverage, much of it generated by its success in reforming such as Jimmy Boyle and Hugh Collins. But behind its formation was the simple theory that the guys who cause most trouble in most jails are the ones with nothing to lose, long sentence inmates with no blue sky at the end of the tunnel. If you have no future, the present hell you live in can't get more hellish – even if you take to attacking prison officers or smearing your cell with excrement.

At the time the Unit was seen as groundbreaking. But the thinking behind it was showing itself as early as the thirties. For the first few years of that decade the Governor was a somewhat controversial figure called R M L Walkinshaw. In those days prison life was truly hard, a punishment. Now enlightened thought is clear that the taking away of your liberty, having every moment of your life ordered, is in itself a huge punishment. But in the twenties and thirties there was little thought given to preparation for freedom or of even little privileges to make prison life more bearable. But Governor Walkinshaw was – as the creators of the Special Unit were to be so many years later – prone to what we would now call 'thinking out of the box'.

Acting without official sanction, he introduced some relaxations in the regime. His liberal interpretation of the prison rules was to lead him into all sorts of problems with the authorities and indeed cost him his job at Barlinnie, and when he was judged to be a bit of a soft touch he was moved to Greenock. At this time prisoners were not allowed to talk to each other when exercising in the prison yard. They walked around silently under the gaze of watchful officers who would stop any chat. This, incidentally, was the reason for the theatrical convention of criminals talking out of the side of their mouth, something the makers of prison films love to exploit. The reason was obvious – the officers from the governor down thought if the inmates were allowed freedom to chat they would use it to plan escapes, attacks on warders they disliked, or even criminal ploys on release. But it is interesting that Jimmy Boyle expounded the view many years later that the initial success of the Special Unit was largely due to allowing the prisoners the opportunity to talk problems through together. Seventy-odd years ago it was not a view widely held, to say the least. But Governor Walkinshaw was of the opinion that turning a slightly blind eye to exercise yard chat would help humanise life in the prison. A clear nod in the direction of the ethos of the Special Unit – treat a man with some decency and you should get some similar respect in return.

To his credit he also introduced games of draughts and cards to recreation time for prisoners. But, again, rather in parallel with what happened in the Special Unit, what you might call 'privilege creep' began to develop and the slightly more relaxed regime in the prison was sowing the seeds of serious trouble.

Another problem was that the prison was by now so close to the criminal stews of the east end of the city. When Barlinnie was built it was out in the country. Now housing was beginning to surround the prison. This was a time of massive gang problems in Glasgow and many of the gangsters had friends inside the 'big hoose'. And most lived in the east end, many now with a daily view of the grim edifice in which villainous mates were doing time as a result of their lawlessness. The prisoners could be seen working in the fields nearby and the quarry, breaking the rocks for bottoming to use in the construction boom in the city. Sometimes, too, outsiders could hear shouting from the inside of the high walls.

The Bar-L was becoming something of an evil island in a part of the city that was growing. One of the problems of this proximity to normal life is that it facilitated tobacco smuggling on a major scale. Disguised drops of cigarettes and so on were hidden in the nooks and crannies around the prison, which the prisoner had access to when working under the eyes of the warders. But even the most efficient officer could not watch all of his charges all of the time. It was not too difficult to collect such valuable booty and smuggle it into the prison. In every prison in the world tobacco was a major problem and the so-called snout barons who controlled it had similar power to that of the drug barons on the outside. They were feared and controlled a sort of prison subculture. Barlinnie in the thirties was no different – access to illegal tobacco caused tensions and fed resentment. The untried prisoners were allowed to smoke when they exercised and indeed one of the warders was in charge of the tobacco box in the yard and opened and closed it at the end of each exercise period. The matches used at these periods lit more than tobacco in December 1934.

By this time official disfavour had led to a new governor being appointed, Captain James Murray. Murray took over a prison where the perception was that discipline had been allowed to slide. Barlinnie at this time was, in that much-favoured cliché of prison observers, a pressure cooker of discontent, and something had to give. The lid was blown off in late December 1934. Earlier in the year there had been signs of what was to come – there had been four escapes involving twelve men. Eleven were recaptured within two days though as an official investigation put it 'one unfortunately drowned on the day of his escape'.

The real trouble began on 21 December. At that time there were around 733 prisoners in the jail. E-Hall was full of what were called 'juvenile/adults' and young men who had been kicked out of Borstals for trouble making or had infringed the terms of their Borstal release on license. The Borstal system was an attempt to keep young first offenders away from adult prisoners. But some of street-hardened toughs who were sent to such institutions were so unruly that they had to be sent to an adult prison.

It was perhaps a bit naive of the authorities to believe that Borstal would scare prisoners off a life of crime on release. Walter Norval, the city's first Godfather, told me when I was researching *Glasgow's Godfather* that on release, and back in Maryhill and up to no good, his time in Polmont was seen as a badge of honour, his spell there adding to his street cred. It in no way scared him off a life of crime that was to include a decade behind bars in Peterhead. So it's easy to see that at the time of the disturbances in 1934, E-Hall with its juvenile/adults had no less of a build-up of pressure than the other Halls. Halls A and B had a full complement of adults, Hall C held the untried prisoners and Hall D was largely empty. The warders numbered just under 100 and the lines of battle were drawn for one of the most dramatic dramas in Barlinnie history.

On 21 December 1934, with the sad, bizarre ritual of a prison Christmas a few days away and a bitter cold seeping into the bones of prisoners and warders alike, the tensions in the prison finally erupted. Without any warning, a large number of prisoners who had been working in the stone yard and nearby work sheds downed tools. They ran shouting and yelling in a ferocious mob in the direction of the yard where the untried prisoners were about to take their exercise and where the tobacco box was held. Knowing what was coming, the warder in charge of the box bravely tried to close it before the advancing mob got to it. It was a vain effort. No chance; he was overpowered by men who were for the most part in custody because of violence. As an angry mob they were a fearsome sight. Like pirates parading sacked booty from a looted ship they ran with the contents of the tobacco box, in a noisy pack, back to the stone yard and workshop area to smoke their cigarettes.

But before they could get back into the safety of the sheds, Captain Murray, now aware of the seriousness of what was going on, promptly ordered the doors locked and the rioters left outside. With nowhere to go, the convicts returned to the stone yards, smoking on the way. But the blood was up and a group of the more determined prisoners went back to the workshop and kicked the doors in and shouted for the men inside to join them in the stone yard. It was pandemonium. The men were screaming and swearing at the top of their voices, pails and other prison bits and pieces were being thrown around. Two warders were chased by the mob through the door leading to E-Hall and the prisoners there broke out to run, again screaming and shouting, to the main group at the stone yard.

By now it was twenty to three in the afternoon. The subsequent inquiry into the events of that bloody weekend reported that much earlier, at around 12.20, one warder had warned the governor of impending trouble in the work sheds and stone yard. Years spent watching convicted men desperately wallowing in the anguish of their situation, filled with resentment and anger, give you a nose for the moment when suddenly the pot boils over. On this day, that warning from an astute warder was to prove valuable. The governor got a message out to warn all staff to 'keep a sharp lookout' for trouble. He also arranged for a reserve posse of warders to be at the ready for frontline action, the group being formed from men on storekeeping and other routine prison tasks.

On hearing that serious trouble had broken out, Governor Murray and a group of officers ran to the untried prisoners' exercise area but by now the rioters had retreated to the north area of the prison. The governor and the warders first went to one of the work sheds where they found some inmates settled and ready to resume work, maybe calmed by a cigarette or two. The officers then ran to the stone yard. Forty-four adults and four juvenile/adult prisoners were there – the toughest of the tough, smoking and lounging about. Many had the hammers used for stone breaking, others knives used in the basket making shed. It was a frightening sight for the governor and a handful of his officers. Murray faced up to the mob with a plea to get them to lay down the hammers and knives. One old lag, who had a bit of respect from the other prisoners, asked the governor:

'Is there going to be a shemozzle?' By this he meant were the warders going to draw their batons and take on the prisoners in a rough house. But at this point, though the troubles of the weekend were far from over, a degree of sanity crept into the situation and the prisoners did indeed lay down their weapons. The extremely brave leadership of the governor had worked. It could have been a bloodbath – the prison staff were outnumbered by around five to one and three of the eleven officers were not even armed with batons. It took real guts to face the mob armed with knives and hammers and plead with them to lay their weapons down.

Eventually this group of prisoners, their hammers and knives cast aside, was marched back to the cells, some still defiantly smoking. It must have been a sizeable tobacco box! Later in the afternoon the governor visited all the halls and sheds and for the moment things appeared back to normal.

All this – what the authorities described mildly as 'a disturbance' – happened on Friday the 21st, though the fact that the weekend approached made little difference to the men who filled the jail; for them one day was much the same as the next. No doubt the governor and his staff debated long their next move and on the Saturday morning around 50 prisoners known to have been involved in the events of Friday afternoon were moved to D-Hall which was more or less empty, with only a handful of cells in use. Two warders escorted each prisoner separately so this time the odds were well in favour of the officers. In D-Hall these men were put into alternate cells, an empty cell between each occupied one.

The fact that it was the weekend did however affect the attitude of the officers. The governor had intended to go in the afternoon to Edinburgh on a matter of a minor family business, not a good idea after the battle of the Friday. And around

1.30 in the afternoon, while the warders were on lunch break and only patrols were in charge of the cells, all hell broke loose in D-Hall. This was a full-blown prison riot. Loud shouting from the men behind bars was accompanied by the sound of glass windows being smashed and tables and furniture in the cells being pounded against the walls. Violent men were acting in concert and venting their anger by doing their best to destroy their place of incarceration in an outbreak of bloody fury.

The governor was still in his house in the prison area at that time and he got an urgent telephone call telling of the alarming violence in the cells. The chief warder, a man called Peddie, was not on the front line when the riot broke out, but he too was phoned and told to get to the prison fast and collect any additional warders he could on his way. It was a fast moving situation and the man in charge on the ground was Warder First Class Bates who headed with a small group of officers to D-Hall, warning them to have their batons at the ready. Unlike the previous day, no one was going to talk this lot of ruffians hell bent on destruction, out of their minds on violence, to submit without a fight. It was a warder's worst nightmare and when Bates and his men arrived on the scene they unlocked and dived into the cells where the furniture and anything else lying around was being smashed. The prisoners lashed out with chair legs and makeshift weapons. The warders cracked batons on skulls. They seemed to have laid into the rioters with such a will that they had subdued them before the arrival of the governor and the chief warder. The busiest man in the prison after that was the medical officer.

There were around 59 prisoners in D-Hall at the time including 11 'Passmen' who were normally well-behaved prisoners with a little more freedom than the run of the mill con. Forty-five cells were badly damaged in the stramash and 41 prisoners treated by the doctor. A handful of warders were also hurt but no one was hospitalized, which seems remarkable given the level of the violence. In the court case that followed, it was claimed that the prisoners in the dock had 'been marked and extremely knocked about'. But it was found that there was no ground to censure the warders who quelled this riot by meeting violence with violence.

But it was no complete whitewash. Sir George C Rankin had been appointed by the government to hold an inquiry into the administration and discipline in the prison. This he seems to have done with remarkable diligence. Governor James Murray and his deputy Captain M P Lothian were officially interviewed as were seven of the prison officers (warders in those days). There were frank discussions with Dr George Scott, the medical officer, the Rev John Hart, the chaplain and Peter Morrison the Catholic visiting clergyman. This was informal stuff with no shorthand notes. John McSporran, the lawyer who represented the 20 prisoners who ended up in court, was also interviewed at length. The 20 who were charged appeared in Glasgow Sheriff Court in January 1935 pled guilty. Mr McSporran, in mitigation, made much of the claim that the untried prisoners had flaunted their privilege of smoking while exercising and stirred up much of the violence. This was not totally accepted by the inquiry which found that the ordinary prisoners would have had difficulty in seeing the untried prisoners smoking. But in fairness to Mr McSporran it was pointed out that on one occasion when he was at the prison there was an incident where this did apparently happen. The inquiry found it not to be the norm.

In court, two of the inmates got six months with hard labour and 18 got three months with hard labour. Seventeen other cons had remission removed. The governor did not escape Scot-free either. His bravery on the first day was highly praised but it was observed by Sir George: 'I regret to say the Governor's behaviour was as bad on the Saturday as it had been good on the Friday.' Captain Murray had not got back on duty on the Saturday until around two, by which time the battle of the cells was over. Likewise Head Warder Peddie was said to have come to D-Hall on his arrival back at the prison but then went elsewhere and did not see what was happening! Looking back, it is not unduly cynical to wonder if it is just possible that there was a touch of the Nelson eye here as it seemed Warder Bates and his boys were crushing skulls and quelling the riot with violent efficiency. And the governor who had acted so bravely the day before was not around to witness what was going on. Was his absence a ploy? The official report, though critical of Murray and Peddie, did not postulate such a stark interpretation.

Indeed Bates came in for praise and was said to have handled the incident most competently. But Sir George was clear when he said that it was obvious that such an incident would lead to claims of the use of undue force and that the Governor should have been there. Instead it was all left to Bates' 'initiative, courage and discretion'. The use of the word discretion in this context is interesting. Murray's excuse for not being on the front line on the Saturday was that he did not think batons would be used. He believed that the men could be calmed without them, a somewhat naive observation considering the level of the violence which, unlike what happened on the Friday, was in full flow when Bates and his men arrived. Batons were indeed used and no one can deny that they were powerfully used – the inquiry heard that twelve of the batons used by the warders broke in their hands. Weak batons, hard skulls.

Sir George made much of the fact that the batons were 'light': 16 inches long and one and a half inches by one and a half, light ash and weighing six and a half ounces. He recommended the introduction of a heavier weapon to crack harder on the skull of any future rioters. There was, however, some sombre logic behind this thinking. The ash batons that broke so easily left the owner wielding a more dangerous jagged bit of wood, and a weapon like that old Glasgow favourite, the broken bottle, was capable of inflicting horrific injury. It was a tough life in the prison service in the thirties.

The quelling of the riot did not lead to an instant solution to all the problems of the Bar-L in those hard days. The prison was back in the headlines in a week or two when one of the rioters tried to cut his own throat with a fragment of crockery. He was patched up and returned to the misery of the cells and stone breaking. But Governor Murray who had, as they say, 'mixed reviews' on his behaviour, got on with the job.

In the early weeks of 1935 he pounded his way round his prison, speaking, it is said, to every one of the prisoners, not an easy task. If the rioters had intended to get their voice heard it seems to have worked. As for the inquiry, it came to the conclusion that smoking inside the prison was largely a red herring and that although the tobacco smuggling was a factor, the pandemonium was created partly by trouble makers and the hard core of gangster inmates partly for its own sake and partly as a plea for sympathy from those outside the walls who could hear what was going on. In fact, it seems the trouble was caused by the same sort of reckless, mindless violent mindset that put the prisoners inside in the first place. It seems the same 'bully boys' who played a role in the 1987 riot had their counterparts back in the thirties.

9

TROUBLE IN THE CELLS, TROUBLE IN WESTMINSTER

Back in the 1880s the satirical magazine *Private Eye* was around a hundred years away from the attention of the reading public. Indeed had the scurrilous fruit of Peter Cook and Nicholas Luard's contempt for politicians and the pompous been around then it would no doubt have been sued, and pursued by those of a censorious instinct, even more than it was in the latter part of the twentieth century. Its editors and writers, London orientated, would not have been sent down to Barlinnie. But as sure as satire is satire they would have ended up in Newgate. There is another certainty – if Glasgow Victorian author James Nicol had been around now he would have starred in one of *Private Eye*'s most popular features. He would have been James Nicol OBN. The Order of the Brown Nose is not awarded lightly, but James Nicol would have been a shoe-in for this honour.

In the early days of Barlinnie, Nicol had been 'by order of the town council' commissioned to produce a book, *Vital, Social and Economic Statistics of the City of Glasgow 1886–1891.* This he did with some serious and meticulously detailed application and produced a volume that was at the time an accurate picture of the city. Reprinted a few years ago by the Grimsay Press it contains some fascinating statistics on the city in general, including a look at the newly built Barlinnie. It points out that the cost of keeping each prisoner was twenty-one pounds eight shillings and eightpence. You couldn't provide much methadone for that! But the Victorian work ethic came into play with the calculation that the profit on work done by the prisoners in a year was one hundred and forty–eight pounds one shilling and ninepence.

Of the prison itself, Nicol wrote, 'It was considered that they [the cell blocks] would suffice for the male criminal population "thirled" to Barlinnie for many years, but already they have been found inadequate, and to ease the pressure, transfers have been made to the general prison at Perth.' That old Barlinnie bugbear again: the doors hardly open and overcrowding is an issue.

This fact was followed by a sentence or two of brown-nosing to the Lord Provost Sir John Muir and his success in a war against crime. Nicol wrote: 'Happily the general record of crime, especially of serious crime, diminishes with the spread of education and the great voluntary labours of our philanthropists amongst the young. Glasgow *per se* is improving every year.'

Nicol would have ensured his OBN with an introduction to his book, addressed to Sir John Muir and the councillors. It pointed out that his book contained 'statistical facts illustrative of the progress of the city, under various aspects, in the last six years, and particularly the results of some of the important work carried out by you.'

It is easy to have some harmless fun with what might be seen as the false optimism, and pomposity, of the Victorians, but the fact remains that at this early stage in the development of penal attitudes there was some positive thinking going on. More recent and less esoteric reports on the prison and the politicians' attitudes to it are less encouraging. For example I doubt if there is a prison in the country that has had more questions asked about it in Parliament. And with the introduction of official inspections, in 1981, and the release of their contents to the media, and the subsequent features and news articles galore, it is all the more surprising that the prison that was a disaster as regards overcrowding more than 100 years ago is still a major problem today. So much so that the files of the city's newspapers are brimming with calls for the place to be demolished. It is still there, however, and will be so for some time.

The sheer volume of criticism of Barlinnie year after year in Parliament and elsewhere makes you despair. And it is not just the conditions in which the prisoners were kept that is of concern. Some of the dangers and difficulties of the staff are also highlighted.

The controversies that frequently pepper the history of Barlinnie have regularly spilled over into debates in the House of Commons, often because of the adversarial attitude of your typical West of Scotland MP. These local firebrands take very seriously their remit to look after the interest of all their constituents, even those, perhaps especially those, who do time in Scotland's largest prison. Any whiff of false imprisonment, any suggestion of bad treatment, has the politicians thirsting, if not for blood, at least for the truth however unpalatable that might be to the authorities. And no bad thing either.

Down the years a frequent thorn in the flesh of ministers was Tom Clarke, a Lanarkshire man through and through, born in Coatbridge and educated in Airdrie and the powerful possessor of both a social conscience and massive Labour majority. When in July 1988 the legendary Speaker Betty Boothroyd announced to the Commons: 'This discussion is coming out of a private member's time, I call Mr Tom Clarke,' a remarkable story of life in Barlinnie 20 years or so ago emerged. Tom Clarke was deeply affected by the fate of a man called Bahadur Singh.

It is worth quoting the exact words of Tom Clarke to show how much the fate of Mr Singh had affected him: 'This debate concerns the treatment of the late Bahadur Singh in Barlinnie Prison. Even as I speak these words, I find it difficult to contemplate that a man of 26 years of age, who lived for a short time in Coatbridge in my constituency and for whom I had been making representations from midwinter until spring this year died on 12 May – the day after his release following six months in Barlinnie Prison. Time after time, as his solicitor took up the case, his friends the Banga family in Coatbridge came to see me and I can still hear them saying, as they frequently did, "they will kill him". Throughout, they had a lack of faith in the administration of British justice which many now think proved chillingly perceptive.'

Mr Clarke went on to pay tribute to the Under Secretary of State for Scotland, Lord James Douglas-Hamilton, as a most humane man with a fine record and an interest in penal reform issues. The member for Monklands West then dramatically increased the pressure on him by saying that 'despite a number of representations and warnings, I can not regard Mr Singh's death on a bus on the way home to the Punjab as a coincidence. There are far wider implications – of civil liberties, of basic human rights, of racism in Scottish prisons and until recent times a lack of Scottish Office concern about the problem. And I believe that these should be urgently addressed.' There was nothing remarkable about how Bahadur Singh had ended up behind bars. No matter what happened to him there – and there emerged two conflicting stories – the tale of how he got there could be repeated in counties the length and breadth of

Britain. Illegal immigration has been a problem for many years and indeed it still is.

There is no dispute that Mr Singh was in Scotland without proper documentation. He had come to work with restaurant owners Autar Banga and Jasbir Banga, but he was reported to the authorities and arrested. At his appearance at Airdrie Sheriff Court he pleaded guilty to a contravention of the Immigration Act and was fined £120. As he had no money on his person he was sentenced to 28 days and sent to Barlinnie pending the outcome of an appeal. Tom Clarke first took up his case in November 1987 as Mr Singh had sought political asylum. The MP was angry both that his constituent was kept in prison while his application for asylum was processed and that the Home Office was dragging its feet, in his opinion, in coming to a decision. But he told the Commons: 'These matters are diminished in importance by the most basic question of all: how was Bahadur Singh treated while he was in Barlinnie Prison?'

Tom Clarke went on to tell the Commons that he had first drawn the Government's attention to allegations of violence against Mr Singh in February (twice in letters to the Minister of State in the Home Office who took a month to reply). During his incarceration Bahadur Singh changed his mind about his appeal from time to time, but the MP said this indecision was due to bullying and abuse in the prison which caused him very great distress. The authorities decided to maintain his imprisonment in view of his previous disregard for immigration control and more allegations of violence and racism were made. The case was then dropped into the Scottish Office in-tray. Mr Clarke said he had written to the Governor, Alan Walker, saying that he had had reports from visitors to Mr Singh of cruel physical and verbal abuse.

Alan Walker had the allegations investigated by a senior manager and his findings were in conflict with Mr Clarke and the Bangas. The governor wrote back to Tom Clarke with words to the effect that Mr Singh speaks virtually no English and it was necessary to interview him through another inmate who acted as an interpreter. In that interview, according to the governor's letter, Mr Singh apparently stated that he had no particular problems at that time and no real fears for his safety although a few slogans had been daubed on his cell door. Mr Clarke disputed that, and remarked he thought the governor himself should have dealt with the problem. He was also unhappy that Mr Walker had implied to the Strathclyde community relations council that there had been no problems with ethnic minority prisoners.

The MP's next step was a letter to the Secretary of State for Scotland which took a month to merit a reply. And the day Tom Clarke got it was 2 June – the same day that in a remarkable coincidence the *Evening Times* had broken the news to his office that Mr Singh had died several weeks before.

Tom Clarke was emotional as he told all this to the Commons. He said he had spoken to the man who had acted as interpreter, Mohammad Sattar, who insisted that in the presence of the governor's representative that Mr Singh had complained about beatings and racist behavior. It was all a bit of a Mexican stand-off. Who to believe? Mr Clarke called for an official inquiry into racism in jails and James Douglas-Hamilton insisted, 'It would be fair to say I have received no evidence that there is any widespread problem of abuse against inmates of ethnic origin in Scottish prisons.'

Tom Clarke wanted lessons to be learned from the death of Bahadur Singh. Maybe no one would ever know now whether on his release he was fit to travel home, or, if he wasn't, had that been the result of what happened to him in prison. But at least in the future there might be better understanding of the problems of ethnic minorities in prisons, regardless of whether or not their incarceration had political overtones.

One swift and successful result of this Westminster spat was that James Douglas-Hamilton was able to report that after the allegations of abuse on Mr Singh, the governor, Alan Walker, held constructive discussions with representatives of the Asian community and had taken a number of immediate measures to help ease the problems which might be encountered by members of the ethnic community in jail. In particular the governor introduced a practice of locating inmates from ethnic communities together for mutual support and companionship and invited the community groups to undertake the translation of the prison's rule book into the four major Asian languages. He also discussed with the community groups visiting arrangements for members of ethnic communities; discussed the special diet requirements of ethnic groups; discussed the need for provision of newspapers and reading material in ethnic languages. All of this was pace-setting stuff at the time and put Barlinnie at the forefront of how the penal establishment should deal with the growing number of ethnic inmates. Even today, this can cause problems.

In Britain, Barlinnie probably has the dubious distinction of having been the subject of more questions asked in the House of Commons than any other prison in Britain. One of the earliest mentions of the prison breaking into the national consciousness concerned not conditions in the prison, but the method of discharge. In 1908 an MP, JG Swift MacNeill, asked the Scottish secretary Archibald Sinclair 'whether he is aware that prisoners, on expiration of their terms of imprisonment in Barlinnie, are not liberated at the gates of the prison, but are conveyed in company in Corporation trams to Cathedral Square, in the charge of warders, and there liberated in view of a curious crowd of men, women and children.' The questioner seemed a man of sensitive disposition and he went on to ask whether prison officials have any legal control over prisoners when they leave the precincts of the prison on the day of their discharge.

He also asked the Secretary of State to consider the advisability of securing the immediate liberation of prisoners at the jail and giving them their fare, or a token, to allow them to travel anywhere in Glasgow. He wanted to know, too, if full regard was being given to the demoralizing effect on the prisoners, who 'whether old offenders, first offenders, or juveniles were herded together in the same tramcar'.

The answer was to the effect that the prisoners were free, although arrangements had been made to take them to the centre of the city by tram. It was said that they left the tram in an open part of Cathedral Square, not far from the other Glasgow prison (Duke Street) and near the Discharged Prisoners Aid Society offices. It was said the prisoners were accompanied by a warder though he was not in charge and that attempts were made to separate first offenders and juveniles from habitual offenders. The Scottish Secretary said that the prisoners were met by friends who he would not call a 'crowd'. This odd tram journey, with its hint of the cattle truck approach, was eventually dropped and prisoners allowed to leave by the main gate. These days you hear of released drug barons being met by mates in Rollers. Changed days!

There is nothing like a reading of House of Commons debates on Barlinnie to get a picture of what the place was like in previous eras. One politician who had much to say about conditions in the prison was the well-remembered Labour politician William Reid in whose constituency, Glasgow Provan, it lies.

Before looking at some of his comments on the life of the inmates, it is fascinating to see, away back in February 1960, an echo of today's comments on the need to bulldoze the place flat.

William Reid suggested to the Secretary of State for Scotland that he should agree to the early demolition of this prison: 'It is now too old to modernise and bring up-to-date.'

He also said: 'This prison has outlived its usefulness. It was built more than 80 years ago. When it was built it was out in the country. Now it is surrounded by housing schemes. The inhabitants of those houses are seriously concerned about the happenings there and the possibility of escapes.'

The 'happenings' mentioned by William Reid are worth recounting. He began his questioning of the Secretary of State, John Maclay, by saying he wanted to call the attention of the House to the state of affairs at Barlinnie Prison, Glasgow. He said that since the beginning of the year, just a few weeks, he had received a large number of complaints – allegations of ill-treatment of prisoners, particularly the treatment of a constituent who wanted to write to him and the concern of folk living near the prison about the dangers of escape. He went on: 'Since the beginning of this year the happenings in this prison, as reported in the press, have been astounding – hooch parties, riots, sabotage, assaults, smuggling of whisky, smuggling of cigarettes, and even a plot to murder the governor.' He further said that this state of affairs was a blot on the fair name of Glasgow and a challenge to the Government to do something about it. He said that the Secretary of State had gone into the allegations and made a straightforward reply that confirmed the allegations 'although we may differ as to the deduction to be drawn from these facts.'

He said that the most serious complaint was about a letter written to him by a prisoner who was one of his constituents.

According to Mr Reid this letter was suppressed by the governor. The local MP's outrage was heightened by the fact that he claimed not only was the letter not delivered to him but the writer was punished for penning it and given six days solitary.

An interesting contrast to all this is the story of peace campaigner Brian Quail's letter on prison conditions in 2001 (dealt with in detail earlier) delivered to sundry politicians, newspapers and fellow activists. On the letter from his constituent, Willie Reid was incandescent: 'Did anyone in this house ever believe that such a state of affairs – dictatorship in its vilest form – could exist in the greatest democracy the world has ever known? Every citizen in this country has a constitutional right to complain to his Member of Parliament regarding legitimate grievances. But the governor of Barlinnie says "not if I can stop it".'

From all this passion and concern it is easy to see why Willie Reid was re-elected time after time. The story of the Letter that Never Was had him in full flow, and it was a sorry picture he painted for his listeners, languishing in plush leather seats 400 miles from the mayhem in the 'Big Hoose'.

When in solitary, the writer of the letter went berserk, or bersie, as the inmates would have it, and broke his cell windows. Willie Reid had some sympathy – 'Is it surprising that such a prisoner being so brutally treated should go berserk?' He went on eloquently to point out that no one in the Commons had a greater respect for law and order than he did but he took the view that prison should be a place for reformation as well as punishment. In his view, good Government would see that prisoners are treated with kindness as well as firmness so that when they leave prison they do so determined to go straight.

Another contributor to this debate was Arthur Woodburn (Clackmannan and East Stirlingshire), a man with an interest in penal reform and good foresight. He recounted a visit to Polmont Borstal in the past when there was a great deal of violence around. He said that he thought that shutting up virile young men in cells at five o'clock at night automatically raised resentment and left them for long evenings with nothing to do but nurse grievances.

He elaborated, touching on some of the philosophy that was later to lead to the forming of the Special Unit – if people are shut in cages they develop all sorts of grievances against society and against the warders. Bad blood develops and 'the kind of violence talked about by my Honourable Friend is the result'. Sometimes a prisoner and a warder become positive enemies just because they get on each other's nerves. He was all for that old favourite of sending the bad guys to some remote island off the west coast and putting them to productive work on the land. It was a dream that might have worked, but the old time-stained walls of Barlinnie still stand and inside still, from time to time, feuds fester.

All this passion from well-known socialists brought a patrician response from Tory John Maclay who tried to put the current concerns into perspective by explaining some of the details behind this particular outbreak of trouble. The start was apparently caused by a 'trivial' matter. It is remarkable how often in retrospect any disorder in the great prison seems to have been sparked off by a minor matter. It is, no doubt, a consequence of the natural tension that always exists between 'caged' men and their captors, however humane the majority of the officers are. This time shirt buttons, of all things, caused the trouble. There was no problem with shirt cuffs or collars that did not fit or did not close properly. Instead, in what John Maclay said was a Hogmanay prank, the buttons were jammed into the locks of some of the cell doors. This meant prisoners

had to be moved to different cells and there were two disturbances but the Scottish Secretary told MPs that the normal
running of the prison resumed on 4 January and that 11 prisoners were punished. Ten of these had their punishments
awarded by the sub-committee of the Visiting Committee and
one was dealt with by the governor.

A few weeks later there was more trouble with a number of
prisoners demonstrating against the regime. This time the
serious nature of the unrest led to the suspension of all
communal activities like work parties, communal dining and
recreation. Not for the first time the prison had been put into
the position where the normal routine was suspended and prisoners locked in their cells.

Explaining all this to the Commons, John Maclay fell into
the trap that from time to time ensnares us all – stating the
self-evident. He said it was obvious that the inhabitants of
Barlinnie are by their nature not the most law abiding of our
citizens in Scotland. Really! But he ploughed on, putting this
particular outbreak of disorder in context by pointing out that
only around 15 prisoners out of a prison population of more
than a thousand had been disciplined.

After he had sat down there followed one of those esoteric
little arguments that the members of the House of Commons
seem to enjoy so much, even to this day. George Lawson of
Motherwell, who had listened carefully as the tale of unrest
had unravelled, was moved to point out that the Right Hon.
Member (Mr Maclay) had spoken of punishments being
'awarded'. Never mind the disturbances, cells being damaged
and missing letters. Instead, Mr Lawson thought: 'it is rather
strange that prisoners should be "awarded" punishment. Surely
punishment is inflicted?' Mr Maclay was not taking this semantic
lecturing and replied briskly that he 'would not like to argue

a point of wording but that "awarding" punishment is a phrase which I have known all my life, certainly since it was awarded to me good and hard. I think it is a normal phrase.'

Whether or not it was inflicted or awarded, in this case prisoners were punished and their punishments were largely decided by the Visiting Committee. Mr Maclay felt that the committee's activities had been perhaps unfairly denigrated to the House and he took the trouble to explain the system. He described the committee as a very important body drawn from a very wide selection of local authorities, men (sic) of the highest integrity. He said they did a difficult job and were completely dispassionate in their approach: 'The governor has the right to report serious discipline offences to the committee and if they wish he can attend any hearing. The committee can have free access to prisoners in their cells or in an area away from prison officers.'

This was linked with the business of the letter that had so upset William Reid. Mr Maclay made a telling point, in much less hysterical manner than his questioner who had ranted on about a vile dismissal of democracy. He said that if a prisoner is to be allowed to use a letter to a Member of Parliament for the purpose of making complaints about his treatment, which he would not be allowed to make in an ordinary letter, and which he had not made to the prison authorities, the result would be that a prisoner could bypass the appointed channels for the investigation of such complaints and could make, with impunity, the most malicious and unfounded allegations against particular officers. This he said seemed undesirable and likely to undermine the authority of the visiting committee. True, but in the case of Bahadur Singh there was real conflict about whether or not he had correctly complained to the authorities before he got his MP involved.

As a newsman I was interested in further comments on this

debate in the press. This spat took place many years ago but some of the comments are in tune with what has tended to happen throughout Barlinnie's history. John Maclay was defensive of the work of the prison staff and said that because they worked so much by way of moral influence and not by repression, and were dealing with excessive numbers, it is not surprising that they have to face Hogmanay pranks or disturbances generally. It is also not surprising, he commented, that discharged prisoners sometimes take exaggerated reports of such doings out of the prison to the press. The old patrician briskly made the comment that 'I think we should keep our eye not on these incidents, but on the wider aspects of criminal justice. I know that it is not easy to do so, particularly with the daily press which is above all interested in news.'

Too true. Down the years the hard-nosed news editors of the Glasgow papers have thrown out a welcome mat to released prisoners with a spicy tale to tell. However sensationally such tales from the inside are presented, it perhaps is not a bad thing if it alerts the general public to what is going on. And it does help raise what was called – even back in the sixties – frank debate.

10

DEATH AT THE END
OF A ROPE

There can be no doubt that the most expert witness who could have been called in any examination of the case for and against capital punishment is the late Albert Pierrepoint, perhaps the most famous executioner in history. A sometime visitor to Barlinnie, he is said to have executed more than 600 people, including 17 women and hundreds of German war criminals. The debate for and against the rope goes on to this day and frequently those who have at any time been involved in the actual process of a legal killing say they are against it and express an opinion that if those who bray for the return of the gallows actually witnessed an execution they would change their minds. So when looking at the subject of hanging, in Barlinnie and elsewhere, Pierrepoint's views on his own career carry great weight.

In his autobiography he wrote: 'All the men and women whom I have faced at that final moment convince me that in what I have done I have not prevented a single murder. And if death does not work to deter one person, it should not be held to deter any . . . capital punishment, in my view, achieved nothing except that revenge.'

And that thirst for revenge is still at large. However not

everyone who has been part of the process of judicial killing is an abolitionist. A little documentary film, *Hanging with Frank* was shot in Barlinnie and won Best Film and Best Documentary in the Reel-to-Reel contest in Glasgow in 1998. Shot in grainy black and white it is a sombre and fascinating piece of work. It features Frank McCue – a former Barlinnie deathwatch officer – with the job of keeping an eye on the condemned man. This was a twenty-four-hour-a-day job shared by three shifts who often sat in the condemned cell drinking tea with the men waiting for the footsteps of the hangman coming to their cell door.

The victim and warders with him would not notice when the executioner spied on them through a secret window to make sure his calculations on the length of rope required were correct. There was an official table to refer to which equated the victim's weight to the length of the rope required, but most executioners liked to have a look at the shape of the man who was to take the drop, just to make sure. Too long a rope and the victim was beheaded, too short and he was strangled to death.

What did they talk about in the condemned cell? Everything and anything other than the obvious – the approaching death of the prisoner – says Frank in the film.

The success of the film is not surprising. The public has a grisly fascination with executions. And the film is compelling and well made. That fascination in the art of judicial killing is well illustrated by the tale of John Amery, the son of the Secretary of State for India in the Second World War, Leopold Amery. John Amery was the first person to plead guilty to treason in an English court since 1654 and died on the gallows in Wandsworth in 1945. It was said that when the two men met in the execution chamber, Amery greeted Pierrepoint with: 'Mr

Pierrepoint, I've always wanted to meet you. Though not, of course, under these circumstances!' Pierrepoint later stated in interview that the two men spoke at length. He said he felt that he had known Amery 'all his life'.

In the award-winning documentary Frank McCue comes across as a world weary, down to earth sort of guy, a man who has lived a lot and seen a lot in his time, a man who would look more at home taking a grandchild for a walk in the park than someone at ease in the Hanging Shed, an expert in the details of executions, a man with total belief in capital punishment. At the time of the film's release he claimed to still be on the list of those wanting to train as hangmen should the rope ever return. He knew Pierrepoint and had had a drink with him from time to time and remembers him as 'as nice a man as you could meet'. He touches on the issue of mistakes being made and innocent men put to death, but in his view if there is 100 per cent certainty then the gallows should come into play.

That talk of certainty is interesting for, in the film, Frank McCue mentions the case of James Robertson, an ex-policeman hanged in Barlinnie, and seems mistakenly to imply that Robertson killed his wife but in fact the victim was his mistress. All very ironic when considering the need to be 100 per cent sure before anyone's neck is stretched. In the film Frank McCue wanders round Barlinnie, remembering when he first joined the prison service in the thirties. And telling all sorts of tales about the grim ritual of execution and happenings in the death cell.

He mourns the fact that so much of the old Hanging Shed was torn down when it finally became clear that the hanging days were over after abolition in 1969. To the old prison warder it was sad that most of the bits and pieces of the executioner's trade had been swept away, the 'end of an era'. He shows the audience the rope used – three quarters of an inch thick Italian hemp – and points out that the actual noose had a covering of finest calfskin and remembers that the noose was placed over the hood on the victim's head to prevent the hood blowing away in the updraft as the victim plunged through the trap. All this detail is delivered in deadpan Glasgow by a grand-fatherly figure, making his testimony all the more horrifying for opponents of capital punishment. If part of the argument against capital punishment is that if you knew the details you would be against it, then this is as near as the layman will get to an execution.

'Hanging with Frank', though a short film, is full of poignant detail, like the fact that the tea in the death cell came 'from a big brown pot' and that there was a constant supply of it. Frank, too, remembers that James Smith, who took the drop in 1952, celebrated his birthday in the death cell and had his cards delivered to him by the warders. He also spends some time in front of the camera at the spot where the bodies of the ten men who died on the Barlinnie gallows lie buried. He shows little emotion as he reels off the names of victims. I, too, have stood there and gazed down on the unmarked graves, noting that you can still see where the stone blocks in the wall of the prison were removed to allow the bodies – the property of the State – to be passed out, dowsed with quick lime and covered with earth. No headstones for these men. I found it more emotional than Frank, especially remembering that in more enlightened times, even with capital punishment still taking place, some of those hanged would have escaped the ultimate punishment because of the intervention of psychiatrists or perhaps, as in the case of James Robertson, the defence lawyer. Robertson's counsel felt the ex-cop made matters worse for himself by not making clear that the victim was a mistress, not a casual acquaintance as he insisted to the jury.

Back in the cells, the film describes the deadly ritual in detail. The beam that secured the rope is shown and it is remarked that Barlinnie could have dealt with three men at a time though all executions that took place were described as 'singles'. We are informed that the bodies hung for an hour over a sandpit to catch excrement and body fluids before being cut down and placed on the post-mortem slab. The fact that the rope snapped the second and third vertebrae and caused instant death is pointed out. Not explored is the belief of some abolitionists that snapping the neck in this way produces paralysis and that strangulation is the actual cause of death, which could possibly be far from instant and painless.

A total of ten executions by hanging took place in the prison's Hanging Shed between 1946 and 1960 (previously the gallows were situated in Duke Street Prison). Ten men had their lives ended by the grim ritual of the rope – the youngest and last being 19-year-old Tony Miller from the south side. Those who died were:

8 February 1946 – John Lyon (victim John Brady)
6 April 1946 – Patrick Carraher (victim John Gordon)
10 August 1946 – John Caldwell (victim James Straiton)
30 October 1946 – Christopher Harris (victim Martin Dunleavy)
16 December 1950 – James Robertson (victim Catherine McCluskey)
12 April 1952 – James Smith (victim Martin Joseph Malone)
29 May 1952 – Patrick Gallagher Deveney (victim Jeannie Deveney)
26 January 1953 – George Francis Shaw (victim Michael Connolly/Conly)

11 July 1958 – Peter Manuel (victims Marion Watt, Vivienne
   Watt, Margaret Brown, Isabelle Cook, Peter Smart, Doris
   Smart, Michael Smart)
22 December 1960 – Anthony Miller (victim John Cremin).

A few of those thrown into the death cell did come out alive.
On occasion the sentence was commuted. One of the most
notorious to escape the drop was double murderer Donald
Forbes who died in Inverclyde Hospital, with two security officers at his bedside, in the spring of 2008. No stranger to the
Bar-L he was once known as Scotland's most dangerous man,
and he was reckoned to have spent 45 years behind bars in
various Scottish jails. In 1958 he was sentenced to hang for
killing a night watchman. But the death penalty was commuted
after Forbes married his pregnant lover in jail. They divorced
and the child was put into care. Forbes was freed in 1970 but
after only a few weeks on the outside he killed again and was
jailed. In 1971 he escaped from the maximum security wing at
Peterhead, but was recaptured. He was released in 1998 and
had a few years of freedom before being branded Scotland's
oldest drug dealer and jailed, aged 68, in 2003 for dealing in
cocaine and cannabis. He was to die before he could taste
freedom again though you could hazard that had he lived it
would have been only be a brief brush with life on the outside
before he was again caged.

The story of every hanging in Barlinnie is a grim one,
murderers of all ages and backgrounds having their life taken
from them by society, legally demanding a life for a life. Some
of the horror has been described in that remarkable film
'Hanging With Frank' but in truth some of the scenes inside
the Hanging Shed defy description or understanding. The last
execution in Barlinnie, that of the 'boy killer' Tony Miller,

illustrates powerfully the battle between the folk who blindly, oblivious to all argument, believe those who have killed, no matter the circumstances, deserve to die in a cold, calculated and fully premeditated way and those who find the concept of judicial murder, and the drawn-out cruelty of it, offensive and sickening.

Though it can be even more cruel elsewhere. In Britain such expert executioners as Harry Allen and Albert Pierrepoint could kill a man or woman around ten seconds after they were taken from the death cell. (Actually the fastest execution on record was performed by Albert Pierrepoint and his assistant Sid Dernley when they killed James Inglis in seven seconds in Strangeways in Manchester in May 1951.) This is in contrast with the torturing behaviour of the authorities in some states of America, where the victim of the gallows, gas chamber, or old Sparky, had to wait for long minutes beside the executioner as the charges they had been convicted of were read to them before their release into eternity.

The life and death of Tony Miller split opinion in Glasgow and Scotland and the only thing of worth to come out of snuffing out a pathetic young life was that it did much to turn public opinion against the rope. Miller had been convicted on 16 November 1960 of his part in the capital murder of John Cremin, a middle-aged homosexual. These days it would be described as a particularly horrible and tragic piece of 'gay bashing'. The murder took place in what was known then as Queen's Park recreation ground. In the sixties in daylight, particularly at the weekends, it was busy with dozens of school and amateur football teams knocking hell out of each other on the ash pitches, activity that meant many hours of work for the doctors in the nearby Victoria Infirmary using wire brushes to sweep the ash and stones out of the many cuts on the young footballers' knees, hands and arms. And during the Glasgow Fair, for a fortnight, the football pitches gave way to caravan pitches and the big top and fairground attractions. The visit of such as Bertram Mills' touring circus was a highlight of life on the south side.

But the 'recce', as it was called, was a more sinister place on dark winter nights. Homosexuals used the bushes that separated it from the railway running from Mount Florida into Central Station in town as a rendezvous. The men who haunted the area on the hunt for a secret assignation in the greenery, hidden from the gaze of passers-by, were easy prey for any strong violent young men wandering into the darkness of the park from the streets of Crosshill or Queen's Park looking for trouble. Cremin had been hit on the head with a piece of wood and robbed of his watch, bankbook and £67. Miller was charged along with an accomplice and both pleaded not guilty but the other youngster claimed Miller had struck the fatal blow, something that it would appear could be a matter of dispute. There were no witnesses. Miller's lawyer, the redoubtable Len Murray, one of the top criminal lawyers of the era, set up an appeal against the sentence of death.

In a book published in 1995, Mr Murray recalled that one of the grounds of the appeal was that the judge Lord Wheatley had failed to offer the jury the option of a culpable homicide verdict, a finding of guilt that did not carry the death penalty. But the court of appeal refused to act and set the execution for just three days before Christmas. Viewed now, many years on, it does seem remarkable that, considering the circumstances and the alleged involvement of two people and the age of the one convicted, that the appeal court took such a hard line on the sentence. At this time there was a growing movement against the death penalty seen by many, and not just liberal writers in the press and pundits on TV, as the ultimate barbarity, a blot on a society that claimed to be civilised.

The opponents of capital punishment rallied in a massive plea for the life of Anthony Miller. On the streets of Glasgow men and women of conscience stopped their last-minute Christmas shopping to sign a petition to save his life. Wherever Miller's family and an army of friends laid down a folding table and handed out petition sheets there were long queues. The fight for a young life was an unforgettable feature of the run up to Christmas. This exercise produced more than 30,000 signatures, a huge, collective plea from the citizens of Glasgow to save Anthony Miller. The petition was sent to the then Scottish Secretary, John S Maclay, and the reply was delivered with Christmas just a week away. With 'regret' Mr Maclay was unable to find sufficient grounds to justify him advising Her Majesty to interfere with the due course of law.

In death row in Barlinnie young Anthony Miller was resigned to his fate. His mother who had fought to save him visited him every afternoon, but he would not talk about the crime. 'It is too late now,' he said. And so at 8am on the morning of 22 December he took his last fateful steps to the gallows. Thankfully he was the last to do so in Barlinnie.

The executioner in this tragic case was Robert Stewart, an Englishman who was on the Home Office list of executioners from 1950 to 1964. He had worked as an assistant to Pierrepoint and had what has been described as the 'distinction' of carrying out one of the last two hangings in Britain when he killed Peter Allen at Walton Prison in Liverpool. What a sad, uncivilised business it all was.

There is an old joke told in prison circles that can make you laugh and think seriously at the same time. It concerns two castaways drifting on an ocean after a shipwreck. They spy an island in the distance and one of them says right away that he will swim ashore. The other worries that they might not get a welcome and could be swimming into trouble, maybe the inhabitants of this unknown island might not be civilised. Of course they are civilised, says the first man: 'There is a gallows on that hillside.'

Interestingly, the first man to die in the new Hanging Shed was, like Tony Miller, also very young, not long out of his teens. John Lyon was convicted of killing a Navy man. His execution was the subject of intense public interest. Though, now that the place of execution had been moved from Duke Street there had been some dilution of the grim ritual. The practice of flying a black flag over the prison on the day of an execution had been abolished with the move to Barlinnie. And the crowds outside the prison at the time of death had also diminished. Around 70 people turned up outside the jail to read a type-written notice pinned on the prison gate at 8.15am, minutes after Lyon's death. It read: 'We the undersigned hereby declare that sentence of death was this day executed on John Lyon, in the prison of Barlinnie, in our presence.' The document was signed by two magistrates, Bailie James Duff and Bailie James Frazier; Robert Richmond, deputy town clerk; JP Mayo, the Governor; Dr Scott, the medical officer and the chaplain the Rev John Campbell. The 70 or so citizens who turned up included the hanged man's younger brother and members of the family. The crowd was allowed by the police to approach the gate in an orderly fashion and read the notice of death for themselves.

The figure of 70 who turned up to 'see off' John Lyon contrasts with the 80,000 (some reports say 100,000) who trekked to Glasgow Green in 1865 to see the last public hanging in the

city. The man put to death by the legendary Calcroft – an executioner infamous for his 'short drops' which resulted in the
convicted man or woman being strangled to death – was the
poisoner Dr Pritchard whose wicked deeds projected him into
Glasgow folklore. His loathsome act of having the coffin lid
unscrewed so that he could kiss the wife he killed goodbye
ensured he was unlikely ever to be forgotten. He also killed
his mother-in-law by poisoning. His infamy was perpetuated
in the wax works of Glasgow showman AE Pickard where for
years he was the star attraction. Pickard also included in his
sideshows a tableau of a working model of a hanging. Whenever
a new murderer died on the gallows, which was quite often,
Pickard changed the clothes on the dummy in the tableau and
labelled it with the name of the most recent criminal to be
executed.

One phrase in the notice of L⌐ ⌐'s death gave a hint of the
barbaric nature of execution: 'I⌐ our presence'. For a hanging
then needed a good party of witnesses, including two magistrates. This necessity led to one Glasgow politician making
history – Bailie Mrs Bell became the first female magistrate to
watch a man killed in front of her when in 1925 John Keen was
hanged for murdering an Indian peddler called Noorh
Mohammed, in a house in Port Dundas. The right for women
over 30 to vote had been won in 1918 (it was to be 1929 before
the legal limit was dropped to 21) and Mrs Bell, when elected
to the council, felt she had to undertake the full range of duties
of a magistrate. Even if it meant the ordeal of watching a
hanging. Keen must have made the ordeal a little easier by
taking his death with great fortitude. Reports said that he walked
to the gallows with a firm step and erect figure.

Opponents of capital punishment are often surprised at the
matter-of-fact attitude the victims of the rope can take. In the

Barlinnie archives there is a handwritten note scrawled in pencil made by a visitor to Peter Manuel shortly before his death which stated that all was more or less 'normal'. And I remember the Glasgow Godfather, Walter Norval, telling me of leaving a court appearance handcuffed to a young man. In the van on the way back to the jail Norval inquired conversationally of this criminal how his appearance in court had gone and his fellow traveller, as it were, calmly remarked that they 'are going to hang me in a fortnight'. It was so matter of fact that it was only when a prison officer confirmed it that Norval realised it was no joke. The youngster he had been handcuffed to was John Lyon.

The most infamous and expert hangman in history, Albert Pierrepoint, was the man who despatched John Keen in the old Duke Street prison and Mrs Bell was a junior magistrate, one of an official party that included another magistrate Dr James Dunlop, the prison governor, the chief constable and the town clerk depute.

It was said in the papers that a large crowd had gathered in Cathedral Square and loitered around for some time before and after the hanging, which took place at the traditional hour of 8am. The newspapers reported that Mrs Bell went through the ordeal unflinchingly and retained full self-possession through this trying experience. She was said to be pale but quite composed when she emerged from the prison after the execution. Interviewed later in her home she claimed not to have been the least upset or nervous at the ordeal, adding that there was nothing in the proceedings to upset any woman possessed of ordinary nerves. Keen had been calm and collected when she saw him in the cells. Immediately after he had replied to the usual question on his identity, the murderer had asked the magistrates if they would shake hands with him. Both bailies agreed to this request and Mrs Bell said the act seemed to afford him some immediate comfort in his last moments. After this the official party went to the execution chamber and they had just taken up their positions when Keen arrived. Mrs Bell said: 'He was pale but carried his head high and went unhesitatingly to his place. There was no scene of any kind.' He was dead 45 seconds after leaving his cell.

All this caused much controversy in the newspapers as the fitness of a woman to carry out such an onerous duty was debated. Mrs Bell seems to have been a woman of real steel. She felt that if a woman offered herself as a member of a town council she should undertake the full range of duties required, regardless of her gender. She added her opinion that any of the woman members of Glasgow Corporation at the time could equally well have undertaken the duty. In the afternoon of the day of execution a formal inquiry was held under a sheriff in the County Buildings where witnesses confirmed what had gone on in the execution chamber and the prison doctor, Gilbert Gerry, confirmed that he had examined the body and 'found all life to be extinct'. A grim ritual indeed.

If Keen took his fate calmly, the same could not be said of the second man to die in the Barlinnie Hanging Shed – a couple of months after John Lyon. Patrick Carraher was a lone wolf bad guy, not a member of a gang, but capable of seriously troubling society on his own. He was convicted of stabbing a man called John Gordon of Aitken Street in the neck. There was an appeal for his life which, considering his 'previous', was not surprisingly turned down. And even such a clearly dangerous, mentally flawed individual – he had been before the High Court twice on murder charges twice previously – had people petitioning to save him from the rope. This would appear to be part of the growing revulsion against the death penalty rather than action in favour of one person.

Carraher was almost your identikit hard Glasgow hard man, always at the ready to flick an open razor across the jugular of an enemy or indeed anyone who crossed him. His defence was mainly that he was a medical psychopath and that the verdict should have been that he was of diminished responsibility at the time of Aitken's death. This was a fairly new track for defence lawyers at the time and it did not wash. But Carraher was a man with no seeming understanding of right and wrong – indeed he was described as a human time bomb who created mayhem wherever he went.

Unlike many of his kind he did not march boldly into eternity. It was reported that this hard man had to be dragged screaming and struggling to the end. It must have been a harrowing morning's work for warders and executioners (there was always an assistant to pinion the victim's legs) alike. Such tales can only strengthen the opinion of those who strongly oppose capital punishment. You often hear supporters of the death penalty say they would carry out the sentence themselves. You wonder if their beliefs would have been strong enough to sustain them on days like 6 April 1946.

One man with first-hand evidence on the effects of participating in an execution was Bill McVey, who had a highly successful career in the prison service, rising from trainee officer to the very top. In 1991, in a remarkable interview, he remembered when as a 25-year-old in Barlinnie, he stood to attention while Albert Pierrepoint placed the rope round the neck of James Robertson. Bill McVey had walked alongside Robertson on the 20-yard journey from the condemned cell to the gallows. As he left the spot he vowed to himself that he would never again take part in such a grim ritual. Pierrepoint seemed able to convince himself that at a hanging he was merely 'the arm of the law' rather than a person taking the life of another. Bill McVey did not see it that way. Subsequently interviewed by a reporter from the *Glasgow Herald* he said: 'It did not turn my stomach, but I remember feeling awful and I believe calls for the return of capital punishment are rubbish.' He pointed out that those who bray loudest for the return of the rope have no experience of it in practice.

The dispatching of James Robertson was even more tragic than most executions, for he could have saved himself from the gallows but refused to do so. It came about like this: he was accused of killing his mistress by running over her with a car (he then reversed over the body several times to make sure she was dead). He was defended by Laurence Dowdall, the lawyer they call the 'pleader's pleader', the most renowned of a long line of Glasgow defence lawyers who have remarkable records of getting bad guys 'aff'. Indeed it is joked that when Rudolph Hess parachuted down on Eaglesham, near the start of the Second World War, and was promptly arrested, his first words were 'Get me Dowdall'. On looking back on the fate of James Robertson, Laurence Dowdall said: 'That was a sad, sad case. The extraordinary thing about it was that if he had told the truth in the witness box he would never have been convicted of murder. His wife knew that he had been conducting this liaison but he said he was not going to let her down in public.

'If he had told the truth and admitted he had this illicit liaison with this woman McCluskey then he would have got off. The very first question the prosecution asked him was "what was Miss McCluskey to you?" He replied: "A casual acquaintance!" The prosecution used this phrase like a knife: every time he mentioned the phrase "casual acquaintance" he turned the knife and it was dreadful to see. Had the jury known of the relationship they might have viewed the killing in a different, more sympathetic light. There could even have been a lesser charge or sentence. But at the trial Robertson would only allow the jurors to see him as a cold-blooded killer of a casual acquaintance rather than a man in a tortured relationship between wife and mistress.'

Laurence Dowdall added: 'Robertson was about 6'2" and by the time counsel had finished with him he looked about 5'2". He would just not admit he had been carrying on with this woman. I saw him three or four days before he was hanged and he asked me to thank Jock Cameron and Manuel Kissen, his defence team, for the work they had done. He also thanked me and said, "I know I am going to hang in three or four days' time, but I am still glad I did not let my wife down in public." It was extraordinary.'

An ex-policeman, Robertson was not in the mould of the stereotyped Glasgow hard man. His immediate predecessor in the Hanging Shed, Paul Christopher Harris, was just that. He was renowned as a fighting man. His story was largely forgotten until the newspapers started to look back at the history of the Hanging Shed on the news that it was to be demolished as part of a modernisation process. Harris's daughter, Mary McCallum, was anxious to find out exactly where his body lay inside the prison. The *Herald* took up the case and their reporter's research indicated that the ten bodies of the men who had died on the Bar-L gallows were buried side by side, wrapped in rough Hessian, along the outside of D-Hall. Sometime in the sixties, after capital punishment had been abolished, the plaques bearing the names of the men had been removed. As part of the capital punishment ritual the victims were denied civilised burial. Their bodies were covered in quick lime and buried in unconsecrated ground.

All the evidence pointed to Harris lying with others including Lyon, Carraher and Peter Manuel. The story of Harris and his brother Claude (Paul Christopher and Claude – odd Christian names for hard men!) says much about the Glasgow slums of the forties and fifties. The brothers had been convicted of acting in concert to kill a Martin Donleavy of Neptune Street. Both had previous convictions for violence. And both were sentenced to hang. Paul confessed to the murder in a somewhat dodgy confession that was criticised by a Scottish Home Department official as 'couched in sanctimonious platitudes not to be expected in a man of Harris's type'. Dodgy or not it was enough to convince the Scottish Secretary to postpone Claude's execution for several days while Paul's death row statements were studied. This resulted in a reprieve. Did one brother sacrifice his life for another? Who knows?

Prison records of the time show that both brothers had behaved with a degree of dignity in the final days and even seemed to have won some sympathy from the prison staff. Paul played the hard man to the end, showing no fear of the rope and urging his brothers who visited him in the death cell to 'be smiling at eight o'clock'. In view of the relationship he had held with the staff on the death watch it is poignant to report that he went to the gallows, not with these men at his side, but with his arms pinioned by officers who were strangers. Paul's confession seems particularly unconvincing due to the victim's deathbed assertion that more than one man had been involved. Maybe then it really was a final act of compassion to save a brother.

It was a sad end to an all too frequent occurrence in those days, a tawdry fight to the death in the worst of the Glasgow slums. Mary McCallum was only 12 or 13 when she learned of her father's fate. Not surprisingly this revelation blighted the rest of her life. It is only to be hoped that finding her father's unmarked grave at least finally brought her some peace.

The most infamous man to die in the Hanging Shed is without doubt Peter Manuel. He breathed his last at 8.01am on 11 July 1958. He was hanged by Harry Allen. Legend has it that Peter Manuel ran the last few yards across D-Hall to his death. Few who were in city at that time will forget it. As the minutes ticked away, hundreds of thousands of Glaswegians watched the clock on their wall, imagining the grim happenings out in the east end. Manuel had in a curious way become part of the city's life. His reign of terror had filled the newspapers for years; his capture and trial had attracted worldwide interest. His death brought a curious form of release to the city. For years there had been a climate of fear nourished by the thought that there was a serial killer at large in the area. But there was still a large percentage of the population against capital punishment. I remember the famous author, artist, and columnist Jack McLean telling of the occasion when as an 11-year-old on holiday in England he asked his father, a stern Calvinist, 'Is this the day they hang Manuel?' McLean Senior sagely made what Jack called an uncharacteristic reply: 'It was a terrible thing which this poor man did, son. But God have mercy on him. We are doing worse.' The sentiment of millions of abolitionists, exactly.

Others would see it as justice. And in terms of the evil he did many thought he simply got was coming to him. Even Manuel himself seemed to in the end accept the inevitability of it all. Strangely Peter Manuel, something of a real-life Walter Mitty, had invented a death penalty background for himself.

In a spell in Peterhead he told lurid tales to fellow prisoners of his father dying in the electric chair in America. The only truth in this fantasising was that the Manuel family had indeed had a spell on the other side of the pond where the mass murderer's father had moved to find work in a car factory in Detroit before returning to Motherwell with his family in 1932. But the fact is that Scotland's most infamous killer had been born in Manhattan of all places. An imagination could run wild on the prospect of what might have happened if Peter Manuel had grown up in the stews of the Big Apple and moved on to the killing fields of the Mafia.

He did enough killing in Scotland, however. In May 1958 he was in the dock charged with eight killings: Anne Kneillands (17), Mrs Marion Watt (45), Vivienne Watt (16), Mrs Margaret Brown (42), Isabelle Cooke (17), Peter Smart (45), Mrs Doris Smart (42) and Michael Smart (10). It was the finding of the body of Anne Kneillands on a snow-covered golf course in East Kilbride two years before that had brought Manuel to the serious attention of the general public, though he had been making headlines since he was a boy – he had convictions for burglary from the age of 12 and was in and out of approved schools. He also showed a penchant for attacking women from an early age. He had confessed to killing Anne Kneillands but since there was no corroboration, Lord Cameron told the jury to acquit him on that particular charge. The verdict on all the other capital charges was guilty. He paid with his life for these killings but, since his death, the total number of his victims keeps getting revised upwards. It seems certain that he also killed a Durham taxi driver, Sydney Dunn, and the usual suspects on the internet speculate that he could have killed up to 15 people. Or more.

The hunting down and trial of Peter Manuel brought into

prominence the remarkable story of William Watt, no doubt not the first innocent man to spend time in Barlinnie, but certainly one of the most harrowing tales of wrongful imprisonment you could find. Ask a prison officer on patrol inside the big house if there are any innocent men in his care and you will get a shrug of the shoulders and the reply: 'Son, they are all innocent in here'. It is recorded that even Peter Manuel in his many stays behind bars brooded alone, loath to mingle with other prisoners and remarkably claiming time after time to anyone who could be bothered to listen that he was innocent.

But William Watt *was* innocent. Not only did he lose his wife, daughter and sister-in-law, shot in the head at close range by Peter Manuel, he found himself in Barlinnie suspected of the murders himself. How it all came about is a story of a series of remarkable coincidences and of police desperation to find a scapegoat, a desperation that not for the first time in Glasgow's criminal history led to an innocent man being accused. The nightmare William Watt endured is horrific. You wonder how anyone could endure the hell of being behind bars in a tough jail accused of murders you did not commit and being reviled by millions outside unaware of the real truth. Ironically, the real killer, Manuel, was in Barlinnie at the same time in a cell not too far from William Watt accused of the less dramatic crime of housebreaking.

When Manuel was on a bloody rampage in the Watts' Burnside bungalow, the head of the house, dubbed by the press the 'Master Baker', was taking a fishing holiday break in Argyll from his bakery business in September 1956. Looking back it seems incredible how a case against him was built up, seemingly without recourse to common sense. The fishing holiday was based at Cairnbaan near Lochgilphead and the police at the time believed he had returned to Burnside on the outskirts of Glasgow to kill his family and then driven back to Argyll to establish an alibi. The impossibility of this is demonstrated by the fact the Watts and Mrs Brown were killed at 6am and that the Master Baker had his breakfast at 8am in Lochgilphead. Even Formula One's finest would find that impossible in a fifties saloon, especially if the long road journey included a river crossing by ferry. In addition, at daybreak in Argyll, William Watt's car was seen parked and covered in frost.

The police were taking too seriously some totally unreliable reports that Watt had been seen driving around Loch Lomondside that night and that he had been on the Renfrew Ferry. They seemed also to ignore the fact that the so called witnesses could not even agree on what kind of car he was supposed to be driving. The fact that William Watt's photograph had appeared in the newspapers, and its effect on potential witnesses, was also ignored. It was all hysterical nonsense and it led to a bereaved father and husband spending 67 tortured days in Barlinnie.

Watt's release and the dropping of charges against him came about in a remarkable way. He had retained the legal services of Laurence Dowdall, as noted perhaps the most successful defence lawyer in Scottish legal history, certainly the most celebrated by the newspapers. Amazingly Manuel, a suspect in both the Watt and Anne Kneillands cases, was in the Bar-L on housebreaking charges, but here he was asking for a meeting with Laurence Dowdall to discuss the Watt case. At the meeting Manuel showed to the legendary pleader that he had knowledge of the inside of the Watt house. He even let slip that Mrs Brown had been shot twice. Dowdall was unaware of this, but when he checked with the police they confirmed it. It seems that Manuel's motive in talking to Dowdall was to plant the idea that someone else had committed the burglary but instead boasted to him about it.

The defence lawyer naturally told the police about the content of the meeting but the detectives on the case did not respond by immediately arresting the serial killer. This was surprising but after one wrongful arrest in the case – that of the Master Baker – they were perhaps overcautious. From what Manuel had told Dowdall there seemed no doubt about his involvement in the Watt murders but, no, the authorities wanted even more evidence. This was a tragic misjudgement since with the killer still at large another five people were to die before Peter Manuel faced a jury. Later in '57 Manuel is believed to have killed a taxi driver in Durham. An attractive Mount Vernon teenager, Isabelle Cooke, was strangled and at New Year Peter Smart, manager of a civil engineering firm, was shot in his Uddingston home together with his wife and young son.

The trial of Peter Manuel eventually began on Monday, 12 May 1958 with the accused shuttling day after day in that famous blue bus from Barlinnie to the High Court with a heavy escort. Manuel had plenty of time in his cell to consider his response to the charges, which ran from mass murder to housebreaking. In his previous life of crime he had shown a keen interest in the law and some ability to defend himself. There were many sensational moments in the trial, but the history of Manuel made it not all that surprising that at the end of the day he would sack his defence team (led by Harald Leslie QC, who later became Lord Birsay). After all, the rope beckoned and the evidence against him was heavy. A man known to enjoy notoriety and limelight grasped a final chance to surprise the court, the press and television reporters, newspaper readers and the hundreds who flocked to the High Court on a daily basis to peer through the railings at the comings and goings and throng the entrance to Glasgow Green, just across the road.

If William Watt's Barlinnie ordeal had not been enough, nor the loss of his family, the monster that was Manuel had not finished with the Master Baker. Manuel was still desperate to convince the jury that Watt had something to hide. Their first joust in court took place before Manuel had fired his defence team. Watt and Manuel, in the dock, were face to face as the Master Baker told of the series of coincidences that cast wrongful suspicion on him, and resulted in that Barlinnie stay. Watt spoke from a wheelchair, which added some poignancy to the legal duel – he had been injured shortly before in an accident. At times Watt broke down and wept and was given water by court attendants. A doctor also stood by. The grilling on this occasion took a tiring two hours. The wrongful Loch Lomondside identification was discussed, as was the state of his marriage and his finances – the total insurance on his wife's life was a mere £50 or £60. He described Manuel's insinuations as a lot of nonsense and the jury agreed.

Later the killer sacked his legal team and it is possible to speculate that one of the reasons behind this act was, as well as the inevitability of conviction, one last chance to torture William Watt face to face. The judge agreed to a re-examination though restricted it to certain points and the Master Baker was brought back into court, still in his wheelchair. The two men stared at each other, a mere six feet apart. It was an electric moment. At one stage the evil mind of Manuel allowed him to suggest: 'Was it not the case that at one stage Watt had said that after he had shot his daughter it would have required very little to have turned the gun on himself?' William Watt was on the verge of a breakdown at this twisted, outrageous accusation and the judge told him to reply merely with an affirmative or a negative. William Watt's loud 'No' echoed round a shocked and silent court. The Master Baker recovered his composure and went on to demolish, to the jury's satisfaction, the farrago of lies and evil insinuation that Manuel was throwing at him.

The trial came to its conclusion and the jury was despatched to consider their verdict. It came at 4.45pm, two hours and 21 minutes after the jury had retired. A bell sounded, the unmistakeable call for all concerned to return to court. Every seat in the place was occupied and people in the overflow stood beside uniformed policemen on duty at the entrance doors. Peter Manuel, soon to face death on the Barlinnie gallows, chatted with police officers in the few moments before the judge returned. There was only one possible sentence. Lord Cameron, the judge, was one of the county's most tough and stern judges, but when he soberly donned the black cap to pronounce sentence of death by hanging he was said to be 'visibly moved'.

The inevitable appeal was later thrown out. Back in the death cell in Barlinnie, Peter Manuel was woken to be told that the Crown saw no grounds for a reprieve. Despite the current distaste for capital punishment you suspect that in 1958 that would also have been the verdict of what we now call 'the court of public opinion'. The news was conveyed to the death cell in D-Hall by Bailie Blas, who travelled from the city centre to Riddrie with the town clerk depute Joseph C Dickson. Bailie Blas undertook this sombre duty in the absence of Lord Provost Myer Galpern who was on holiday. Only 12 people were outside the prison at one minute after 8am as Harry Allen activated the drop and the monster died. The first official indication that the execution had taken place came at 8.50, by which time there were 30 people milling around the gates when Bailies John Paterson and John Macdougal left the prison.

Asked if Manuel had said anything before his execution Bailie

Paterson said 'No' and Bailie Macdougal said, 'He made no reference to anything.' The local politicians then said the hanging was carried out in 'a satisfactory and expeditious manner'. So ended the life of a serial killer.

11

THE BSU – SO SUCCESSFUL
THEY SHUT IT DOWN

With the possible exception of the execution area, aka the Hanging Shed, the most famous part of Barlinnie is, or was, the Special Unit. Here, for around 20 years from the early seventies to the early nineties, was conducted one of the world's most important and controversial experiments in penal theory. The experiment was followed by all those interested in rehabilitation, especially the rehabilitation of murderous hard cases who had been transported into the toughest of jails, with the keys figuratively thrown away. Its place in history is secure. But if you visited it today you would be significantly underwhelmed. The small area that held such infamous prisoners as Jimmy Boyle, Hugh Collins, TC Campbell and Larry Winters is now mainly used as a storeroom. The cells, once partly the cause of huge criticism because the lifers were allowed to add some little touches of home comfort, like a battered armchair, are now the repositories of prison service paperwork, cardboard boxes piled high. You can't get more mundane than that.

It is a remarkable, stop-you-in-your-tracks moment actually to see the Special Unit for yourself these days. Back in the seventies on the streets of Glasgow, if you had listened to pub talk, or even read some apoplectic broadsheet columnists, you might have got the idea that life in the Wendy House or the Nutcracker Suite, as it was variously nicknamed, was a cross between the five-star luxury of the Beverly Wilshire in LA and the Grosvenor in Mayfair. Garbage.

To the visitor now the first impression is how small it was and how impossible it must have been to have had any real comfort in it, never mind so-called luxury. The officer-to-inmate rate was much higher than in a normal nick. But the food was not much different from prison fare, no Gordon Ramsay stuff, despite the talk on the streets. Though the freedom to do a little cooking did give the Special Unit an occasional touch of experimental cuisine. I remember Stuart McCartney, one time of the *Express* and the legendary doyen of crime reporters in a city with hundreds of scribblers who specialise in following the doings of the bad guys, returning from a visit to the Special Unit and telling me how he was invited to taste curried porridge. It was not an experiment that 'Bullet', as McCartney was known, voted a success.

From the day it opened the Unit was a test bed. A small group of long-term prisoners, generally serving 15 years or more, were held together in a separate secure area inside the main prison, but given a much more relaxed regime than that of prisoners held in normal cells. Prisoners in the Unit wore their own clothes, had record players and their own personally owned books rather than the prison library's tattered paperbacks. Freedom, responsibility and a degree of personal choice were all watchwords in an experiment that bucked the thinking of most of the people at the top of the conventional prison hierarchy. Even mail was uncensored. It is not rocket science to predict that no matter how successful it would be in reforming individual villains that elsewhere in the prison system there would be serious resentment and the belief that if you wanted to share in this new regime then the worse your crime the better your chance was. It is understandable that some officers in the mainstream saw what was going on in the Bar-L as an invitation to prisoners to become so disruptive that they had to be moved out of the rigid mainstream regime to the new experimental 'cushy' Unit.

And, of course, rumour and exaggeration prompted some folk to start questioning what was really going on. Even the police found some of the results of this experiment hard to take. And hard to understand. Les Brown, who went on to become one of Glasgow's most famous detectives, told me what, to the cops, was a maddening incident souring any positive thoughts they had about the Unit. He arrested a guy for shoplifting and this villain, when asked where a TV he had stolen was, calmly remarked that he had handed the stolen property in to the Special Unit. You couldn't make it up, says Les. Brown however was not easily put off and despite warnings from his superiors in the CID to let it go, he asked the then governor of Barlinnie to give him the make and number of the set to help identify it. He got a call back from the then top man Mr Hendry to inform him that a) the set was no more as it had been smashed, and b) he had no control over the Special Unit anyway! Hints of what was to happen over the years.

The BSU, as it was formally called, was the result of the thinking of many people in the prison service or with a particular interest in penal matters. The official report on its closure in 1994 comments: The Barlinnie Special Unit opened in February 1973 on the recommendation of a Scottish Home and Health Department Working Party, which was charged with considering 'what arrangements should be made for the treatment of certain inmates likely to be detained in custody for very long periods or with the propensities to violence towards staff.' The recommendation said that: 'A Special Unit should be provided within the Scottish penal system for the treatment of known violent inmates, those considered potentially violent and selected long-term inmates' and 'the traditional officer/inmate relationship should be modified more closely to a therapist/patient basis, while retaining a firm but fair discipline system.' Optimism of a high standard.

Incidentally that final report plucked a couple of quotes from the hundreds of academic investigations to show the diversity of opinion on the BSU. They included: 'One of the most imaginative and enlightened experiments in penal history' (Kennedy, 1982) and '. . . the easiest, plushest prison unit that has ever existed' (Conlin and Boag, 1986). The latter quote seems a bit over the top and also seems not to have taken account of the country house hotel ambience of some of England's open prisons. Indeed all the academic comments on the achievements of the Unit can create a little head-scratching to the outsider: it was so successful they closed it down.

It was intended right from the start that the Unit would operate as a 'therapeutic milieu', staffed by a combination of Discipline and Nurse officers and where the emphasis was on 'treating' those who had behaved, or were suspected likely to behave, in a violent manner. The final report in 1994 acerbically noted that at no time did the 1971 working party suggest that the Unit should function as a 'community' and that 'it would seem that this element of the Unit's ethos came about more by accident than design'. All this came at the end of the experiment, though the use of the description 'experiment' for something that lasted around 20 years seems a bit odd.

The frequent use of the word 'treatment' in the BSU story is interesting in the context of Barlinnie's history. At one time treatment was breaking rocks in the nearby quarry. Mind you, looking at penal conditions worldwide, Barlinnie, even in the bad old days, wasn't as harsh as what went on in America. I remember in Florida just a few years ago watching prisoners in a chain gang cleaning out roadside ditches that were the habitat of 'gators – watched over by prison officers with rifles – a bit more tough treatment than making baskets in the warmth of the Bar-L work sheds! Incidentally this chain gang in the States was working out of a prison called Copland Road, a name with an affinity for any Rangers fans doing time in Barlinnie.

One of the early brains behind the visionary concept of the BSU by the prison service was a small, quiet Aberdonian called Ian Stephen (not to be confused with Alex Stephen, a high-ranking civil servant who had much to do with the nuts and bolts of setting the Unit up). Ian Stephen went on to become one of Scotland's leading forensic psychologists. Indeed he worked as a consultant on the highly praised TV series *Cracker*, starring Robbie Coltrane. Ian Stephen is on record as acknowledging the difference between TV crime and the reality. Fans of the series will be interested to know that: 'The Cracker character was really nothing like what real forensics is all about. You could not survive in the extreme way he did – the police would not use you.' He went on to point out that the series, which attracted 14 million viewers at its peak, brought forensics to the public attention and that of the press.

Ian Stephen studied psychology at Aberdeen University and after leaving found himself teaching languages at a Borders school. The experience re-ignited his interest in psychology and he began working with young offenders in Glasgow – no shortage of interesting cases there. Interviewed on his work he told one reporter: 'If you can work with these kids you can work with violent men. The kids are far worse.'

Stephen is proud of the work he did in the BSU. He was the only psychologist working in the Scottish prison service at the time. There was genuine concern that the removal of the death penalty had inflicted desperate men on the prison community. Often without the slightest chink of hope in their lives they were attacking prison officers and each other, taking any and every opportunity to break out onto prison roofs to throw tiles at the warders below. They had nothing to lose. Cells were smeared with excrement and mattresses set ablaze. Prison officers were subjected to repeated attacks.

Stephen and others thought there must be a better way and the seed that started the BSU experiment was planted. The man who some say was the prime mover in turning the idea that 'something must be done' into reality was Ken Murray, who died in 2007 aged 76. Former Labour cabinet minister Brian Wilson described him as 'one of the most significant advocates of penal reform in the latter part of the twentieth century'. And Murray was no ivory tower theorist – he spent 28 years in the prison service. Even in the early days of his career he was of the belief that there must be better ways of treating violent offenders than punitive incarceration.

For years the Special Unit was at the receiving end of public hostility and regarded as a soft home from home for evil men, generously provided by the taxpayer. There were lurid stories of sex and drugs behind the walls of the BSU but Ken Murray was its most public face, defending the experiment against a massed army of armchair critics. And there were plenty, especially since the famous inmates like Boyle, Collins, and Larry Winters were seldom off the front pages of the tabloids. Boyle and Collins are still high profile but the Larry Winters story has less resonance these days, his sordid death in the BSU now largely forgotten by the general public. But it is as intriguing as any tale to come out of Barlinnie.

Winters and Boyle both sparked films, *Silent Scream* and *A Sense of Freedom* which involved Glasgow actor David Hayman: he directed the Winters story and played Boyle in *A Sense of Freedom*. Powerful work from the Citizens Theatre star who went on to become one of the biggest names in television. While Boyle and Collins enjoyed a measure of fame as sculptors, inside and outside Barlinnie, and as the perfect examples of the redeeming nature of the Unit and then went on to productive lives outside of prison bars, Larry Winters never left Barlinnie alive. He was found naked and dead on a chamber pot in the Special Unit in 1977. Winters, like Boyle and Collins, had a rough childhood and criminality was involved from an early age. It ran in the family. It is interesting that so many of the young men who ended up in the Nutcracker Suite had such violent childhood backgrounds. Winters went down the usual road of many brought up in his milieu – assaults and minor crime and violence leading to the act that finally put them behind bars for long sentences. His career is a useful case study in the ongoing nature versus nurture argument that keeps academics interested in the penal system busy.

Larry Winters shot a barman in Soho in 1963. He was caught, tried and, as the tabloids say, caged. The use of the word caged, a favourite of headline writers, has resonance with cause and effect in criminality. This is underlined by Jimmy Boyle's claim that he was 'animalized' by the prison system before he was moved from 'the cages' in Inverness to the Special Unit. The description gives us some insight into the mind of the long-term prisoner and why some fight their depression, and the feeling of being 'animalized', by fighting everything around them, even behind bars. Boyle concedes that such as he, Larry Winters and Ben Conroy ended up in the BSU as a result of 'being difficult to control', which is a masterly understatement. In P-head and Inverness they and such as TC Campbell were a nightmare. Desperate men inside do desperate things, but many confined themselves to throwing the odd cup of boiling water at the inmates they call the 'beasts' – the criminals in for child assault and other crimes of a sexual nature. But in Peterhead there was a hard core of guys who would attack anything that moved. Their lives were a shocking mix of stabbing warders, riots, and 'dirty protests' – as the practice of urinating and defecating everywhere and anywhere was called. As mentioned earlier, this 'hopeless aggression', shared by a handful destined to spend long years without hope of release, was one of the reasons for the BSU in the first place.

There is still controversy around the drugs that killed Winters and allegations that he had become addicted to anti-depressants fed to him by the prison system to wipe out the 'difficult to control' side of his character are still made. But perhaps it should not be forgotten that allegations of illegal use of recreational drugs smuggled into the Unit have never been totally dismissed. Whatever the truth, his end was as sordid a tale as you can get. The London barman had been killed to get a fiver by a man with a proven IQ way above average. In Peterhead, where Winters spent time, his obvious intelligence went unnoticed, its potential ignored.

It was a different story when he was transported down south to the then new BSU. There he met Bill Beech, a member of the so-called creative-artistic caucus who regularly trudged through the uninspiring surroundings of Riddrie to 71 Lee Avenue to go through the rigours of security – at times the visitor might think it as hard to get in as get out – and on to the Special Unit, there to dispense artistic advice and that rare ingredient in prison life – hope. As was intended, the Unit gave Winters a sense of purpose unknown in his life up to that point and he began to write. Beech was quoted as saying: 'If Larry had lived I think the writing would have flourished. That's the marvellous thing about the Unit. It was just a relief that he could actually sit down and write and relate to things. But the drugs he took masked all that. He was still in prison and facing the rest of his life there.'

As far as drugs are concerned, Winters certainly had an extensive knowledge of the subject but it is something of a mystery how a man who knew all about tolerance levels became so careless that he killed himself. Not surprisingly his death led to a public frenzy about the notoriously liberal regime in the Unit at that time. And there is no doubt that the use by inmates of drugs brought in from the streets played a role in the eventual decision to close the Unit. No matter the argument and the blame shifting, the fact is that in the case of Larry Winters a human life had been snuffed out.

But amid tragedy there was hope and progress unthinkable in a normal prison unit. For a spell the BSU even had its own little newspaper produced by the inmates. It was called, aptly, *The Key*, a title with all sorts of connotations – the key to freedom, the key to artistic fulfillment, and the key to keep you locked away or to unlock you. Sprinkled among the longer articles were short poems, little pearls of wisdom. Many were moving. And one, unsigned, would have made a poignant final end piece to the Larry Winters story:

Mentally and physically alert
How long must I writhe
In this house of tormented souls.

I have read of writers comparing life in jail with that of a boarding school. I most certainly don't see it myself, but I suppose there are some vague similarities if you look hard enough. Certainly *The Key* had the look of a school magazine, typed on a battered machine and the pages run off on a copier that could have used more ink. No colour spreads, no dramatic typography. No adverts for holidays in the Seychelles, of course. The content itself was far removed from school mag stuff. There was some moving writing on the plight of long-termers and bits and pieces of comment on prison life gathered from publications from around the world. Much writing on the evil of capital punishment was featured, not surprising since within the walls that contained the Special Unit ten men had died at the end of a rope. Plenty, too, to interest those studying the effect of long-term confinement on the human condition. Lots of poetry, of course, and much brain wringing about how each particular writer had ended up in the BSU. Many of the pieces gave insight into the thinking of prisoners in the Unit taking part in the groundbreaking experiment in prison reform. It is very moving to read in *The Key* of Boyle's first encounter with a lump of clay and the reward of sculpting it into a work of art.

From Issue One there was agreement from the prisoners who produced it to invite contributions from non-prisoners. One of the first was from Father Anthony Ross, a former Chaplain of Edinburgh University who at one time was vice-chairman of the Parole Board in Scotland. Ross had been raised as a Free Presbyterian, but converted to Catholicism and went on to become something of a controversialist. A hugely charismatic intellectual, he had a lifetime interest in crime and punishment. His contribution to the first issue of *The Key* was a wide-ranging piece discussing the role of the clergy in prison, acknowledging that some prisoners liked to receive the sacrament while others were more interested in debate with social workers.

The first issue also featured what was to become a constant hobbyhorse, allegedly irresponsible and inaccurate reporting of the Unit in the press. Another major theme was to repeatedly emphasize the belief that if an offender is treated like a person rather than a piece of trash rejected by society, then the offender will reciprocate. It was a serious nod in the direction of accepting the thinking of the founders of the Unit. It is interesting that long before the Unit came into being and long after it had been closed, similar thoughts were around, notably in the thirties at the time of the tobacco riots and more recently when Paul Ferris, as recounted earlier, made similar comments about a more relaxed regime in the Bar-L segregation area.

David Scott, one of Scotland's most lauded journalists who often worked on crime stories, knew the Glasgow scene better than most. He was part of the team, including Joe Beltrami and Ludovic Kennedy, that fought for years to overthrow the wrongful conviction of Paddy Meehan. He was a natural choice to be asked to write for *The Key* and was told that he could be as blunt as he liked. Right at the start of his piece, in November 1974, he said: 'It was with some dubiety that I agreed to write an article for *The Key*. Not because I believe the magazine is a bad idea. Quite the contrary. I think it was because as a former "hard liner" who once advocated capital punishment for certain offences, my ideas are now less well defined and I am not

exactly certain of what I believe in.' As honest and blunt a statement as the little magazine's editors could have wanted.

He went on to point out that if capital punishment had not
been abolished, some of the six men then in the Unit would
not be alive. 'There are some I know who would say "so what?"
to that. But it is a fact that the law, as defined by politicians in
the House of Commons, has to be carried out far away from
that somewhat cosy atmosphere. And it has to be carried out
by people who often have little or no say in what the law
should be. It is easy for those who live and work outside
prisons to ignore the problems within. It is also simple for us
to recognize the problems and just leave it at that. After all, we
can walk away from them at any time. But officers and prisoners cannot. They have to live with the situation created by
the abolition of capital punishment and the fact that many
long-term prisoners may well be there, if not for the rest of
their lives, at least for many years ahead.'

When David Scott penned his thoughts there were only six
men in the Unit and they were said by the press to be the most
dangerous prisoners in Scotland. He observed that three may
have been disruptive but that 'only two could properly be
described as dangerous'. He went on to remark: 'There are
always two sides to every story, but whatever the rights and
wrongs in the circumstances surrounding the assaults on staff
that these two were involved in, one thing is certain. And that
is they have taken everything the Scottish Prison Service could
throw at them. It seems to me that these two were at a stage
when they had absolutely nothing to lose. And if a repressive
penal regime continues to breed violence, it stands to reason
that officers are going to be hurt, or even killed.'

Scott went on to ponder whether a solution being experi-
mented with in jails south of the border was the answer. There,

a fearsome regime called the Cooler was being tested and the suggestion was that is was more effective than the 'soft' option of the Special Unit. Troublemakers sent to the Cooler had to 'behave' for 180 days before being allowed back into the normal prison regime. Scott reported, 'In this situation you are a separate unit responsible only to yourself. There you win or lose by what you do. If you misbehave no one suffers but you. In the Special Unit it would seem that the inmates do have a lot to lose. They have a responsibility, not only to themselves, but to others too. One wrong, irrational or impulsive move could ruin this experiment. It could mean goodbye to a situation where some kind of human existence is offered for the many years of imprisonment that lie ahead. It could mean goodbye to the chance of proving one can be rehabilitated in a system which, in the main, is not geared to this type of work. And it could also mean goodbye to a real opportunity of eventual release, not only for the errant inmate, but for others in the Unit, and for those who might have followed.' Any man who destroyed that concept would have to live with a heavy conscience.

Scott ended this astute piece of journalism by saying that if it appeared he had been arguing a case for the Unit he had not consciously done so. He added, 'What I do believe is that the crimes committed by the five who have been there most of the 22 months that the Unit has existed were dreadful and that there was no possible excuse for them. Indeed it is only fair to say that four have offered no excuse. All have however expressed regret and sorrow. (One continues to protest his innocence.) I believe I have seen a dramatic, almost unbelievable change in outlook by one of the men, whom I have known professionally over a period of years. There are those who say they [the Unit's inmates] deserve a break, that they have suffered enough

over the years. My natural instinct is to say so have the relatives of their victims. But I have not visited them and that might
be a story for another day.'

He ended his perceptive observations on the early days of
the BSU powerfully: 'The Special Unit has had teething problems. No doubt it will be the object of further public criticism.
Despite this, I am persuaded that it is making a valuable and
long-overdue contribution to penal reform in Scotland. Having
met and got to know officers and inmates, I wish both groups
all success. They will need it.' Too true. Public criticism rained
down on the Unit for almost its entire existence, a constant
corrosive poison that in the end contributed much to its demise.

Another of Scotland's most famous reporters, Stuart
McCartney, a long time *Express* man, wrote extensively on his
visit to the Unit – a visit that came about because the prisoners
wanted the press to see for themselves what the place was like.
Stuart wrote that the men in the Unit were members of the
world's most exclusive club, a grouping of the most dangerous
men in the Scottish prison system, a motley collection of killers
serving life for murder or manslaughter. This club was for
dangerous men only. What he saw when he met the members
of the 'club' astonished this vastly experienced journalist. Here
he was having coffee and biscuits with men, many of whom
he had seen sentenced, a reporter watching as they defiantly
laughed in court when sent down. Now he listened as one of
the hardest of the hard earnestly told of his ambition, on release,
if ever he was to be released, to devote his time to helping the
youth of the Gorbals. Another, a villain Stuart had tagged as
beyond redemption, said that in the Unit he had found hope
for the first time in his life.

Alex Stephen, Prison Service Controller of Operations, and
one of the real driving forces behind the formation of the Unit,

told the *Express* man that the prison service had to find ways to handle long-time violent prisoners, especially as capital punishment had been abandoned and hopeless lifers with nothing to lose were wrecking the system with dirty protests and attacks on prison staff. 'We had to decide when setting up the Unit how a man would react when he realised that eventual release was unlikely, or at least so far distant as to be meaningless. How do you rehabilitate someone who may never get out?' Alex Stephen was too wise a man to claim instant success but he pointed out that in the first ten years or so there had been no serious assaults on prison officers.

The prisoners were equally straight, with Stuart once saying: 'I came to know myself in here. I never thought I could be the type of human being I am today. I have matured in here and I know my maturity came too late. I can only pray to God that someday I will get out.' Another dangerous man in this exclusive club said with insight and realism: 'If it had not been for this place I would have been dead. Or OTHERS would have been.'

That little magazine, *The Key*, was itself, of course, controversial. What aspect of the BSU wasn't? The first issue had a "print run" of 750 and it seems it was a sell-out. Though that doesn't look quite so good when it is considered that most of the sales were at an exhibition of prisoners' art at the Richard Demarco Gallery in Edinburgh and that most of the buyers were foreign visitors. This was not really the intention. The real purpose was to open minds inside and out of the BSU as to what was going on there and what it could lead to in the way of prison reform, and to stimulate debate. The second issue ran to another 750 copies but it seems it was mostly bought by officers rather than inmates; maybe the arty tone was too much for prisoners brought up in the Murdochised world of Page

Three 'stunnas'. And some governors were not too keen to have it distributed on their premises. To some these few sheets of paper stapled together and giving the caged intellects of the Unit space to dispense their ideas was seen as a threat to authority. *The Key* only ran to three issues.

I suppose you could say that the magazine was something of a collective work of art by the inmates of the Special Unit, but of course it was the sculptures of such as Collins and Boyle that gained the most attention. There was huge optimism about the Unit in its early days. That optimism and a feeling that not only was this pioneering penal work but that it was bound to succeed and last comes strongly out of reading '*The Special Unit – its evolution through its art*' produced by Glasgow's Third Eye Centre in 1982. Ludovic Kennedy called the book 'the inside story of one of the most imaginative prison reforms ever attempted'. And the sleeve quoted both Nietzsche and an unnamed Special Unit inmate. The philosopher opined: 'The broad effects which can be obtained by punishment in man and beast are the increase in fear, the sharpening of the sense of cunning, the mastery of desires; so it is that punishment tames the man, but does not make him "better".' The prisoner said: 'This place is a big mansion house with a hundred different doors in it. Each one you open up there is a different scene inside and your mind starts to open up. . . .'

Of that there can be little doubt. The Special Unit did open minds. In the general run-of-the-mill prison establishment there is an old saying that you can only help those who want to help themselves. And that even applied to the Special Unit with its handpicked inmates. Barlinnie governor Alex Thomson said in 1981 that 'the move [of violent prisoners to the Unit] is not always successful. One or two men have had to be moved back to ordinary prisons either because they couldn't cope with the pressures the Unit puts on a man or because they were not responding.'

In an interview with the *Sunday Post*, Mr Thomson, who moved on to become principal of the Scottish Prison Service College after three and a half years in charge of the Unit, gave Glaswegians an interesting view of the prison within a prison. The *Post*'s many readers were told that 'There are four standard cells seven feet wide and ten feet long on two landings, one above the other, and looking on to a corridor about 15 feet wide. Outside there is a room about the size of two living rooms which is used as a TV and communal room, a small kitchen, a couple of offices used by staff and a communal ablutions room. [The cells still had chamber pots, as did the rest of the prison, as slopping out was the norm.] There is an exercise yard the size of a tennis court and a small garden and greenhouse, all separate from the rest of the prison. The Unit has its own security system.'

At this stage in its development the Unit had three officers always on duty to supervise the eight prisoners. Allowing for shifts, holidays, illness, etc, this meant that there was a staff of 18. The officers in the Unit were specially selected for the job though any officer in the prison service was allowed to apply for a week's work in the Unit to find out how it worked. The routine involved unlocking the cell doors on weekdays at 6am and locking up each night at 9pm. At weekends the unlocked hours were 7.30am to 5pm. Prisoners were allowed to wear their own clothes and have more or less unlimited visits. There was no work programme though the prisoners cleaned the area themselves. There were no duties but each man was expected to create a programme of study or other work. This worked well in the early days with such exceptional men as Winters, Collins and Boyle involved in artistic enterprises, but in the final years critics were complaining about prisoners who slept in till midday and spent the afternoon with visitors and then lay about watching TV at night.

The founding ideas of giving these desperate men responsibility and respect led to meetings galore and much discussion. On Tuesdays the governor, prisoners and staff gathered under an elected chairman who could be a prisoner. The idea was that anything relevant to the Unit could be discussed. There were also informal meetings on Fridays and special meetings to cope with problems that had turned up as well as group meetings where prisoners with personal problems attempted to work them out with two of the staff and two other prisoners. The point of these seemingly endless talking shops was to teach prisoners social responsibilities, often for the first time in their lives.

Since they were out of the mainstream prison system and denied the chance to earn money in the workshops, the BSU prisoners were give a 'wage' of £2.09 to buy tobacco, sweets, papers, toilet articles and so on from the canteen. Once a week a prisoner – chosen by the committee – was allowed into Glasgow under escort to buy items unavailable in the prison and approved by the governor. In an interview, Governor Thomson was realistic enough to say that it was too early to make a judgement about success or failure. Too true, as the experiment had another ten years or so to run. But he did point out that in 1981 none of the five men who had been through the Unit and released had 'been in the least bit of trouble'.

So much for the nuts and bolts of the Unit. But its founders and chief protagonists had much more high-flown hopes and ideals. In a deep piece in *The Special Unit – its evolution through its art*, clinical physiologist Ian Stephen looked at the role of education in the Unit. He found it vital that a prisoner in the

Unit was enabled to develop 'skills and abilities which are latent but unexpressed within him'. He pointed out that although intelligence is not one of the criteria for admission to the Unit, nearly all the prisoners who have passed through it are of at least average intelligence and 'a large number have fallen into the superior range, i.e. the potential to achieve degrees at university level, had social and educational experiences permitted'. The number was said to represent a significantly higher proportion than can be found in the general population. When the book was published, three prisoners were studying with the Open University, others had undertaken O Grade courses, one was involved in a short-story writing course, music was being studied and, of course, the Unit's involvement in sculpture at the highest level was ongoing.

It is interesting, too, that Ian Stephen points out that the decision to allow the prisoners to design their own work study programmes, something much criticized by those agin the ethos of the Unit, was valuable. He pointed out, 'This is no easy task when one has been accustomed to others laying down daily work schedules for you and requires considerable discipline and responsibility.' This lavishly illustrated book – the pen and ink drawings of Hugh Collins in particular are hugely impressive – is an antidote to some of the hysterical vapourings of the tabloids. The Unit may have lost its way in the end, but this book intriguingly charts at least part of the journey to ultimate closure. Ludovic Kennedy perceptively writes of the hard men such as Collins, Boyle, Winters, Bob Brodie and Tom Galloway: 'It is no surprise that they proved to be talented; for they were or are all men of unusual energy, and one can see now that their capacity for violence was the distaff side of their capacity for creativity.' Yet he goes on to say that the attention paid to the artworks of the prisoners may well have blinded some to the Unit's primary aim, which is not acclaim for the art but therapy for the artist. In his view what the Unit was doing was to give men whose psychological growth had, for one reason or other, been stunted, the opportunity for self-discovery; and by so doing to change fundamentally their attitude to society.

In books like *The Special Unit – its evolution through its art* and also in *The Key* there is optimism and honesty from both sides of the argument. The short-lived little magazine even ran a critical article by a prison officer who vocalized the concern of the man in the street who feels that when the Unit is written about there is too much praise for the artworks and not enough regret and concern for victims. This lack of concern about the victims was, of course, a criticism also made by David Scott. The prison officer who penned his little piece also criticized Jimmy Boyle for not taking the opportunity in Peterhead to attend classes on art. This seems a fair point, as even in the seventies there were good educational opportunities in most prisons. But you can only, as they say, help someone who wants to be helped. And the Special Unit did create that desire in previously violent men and that must surely be seen as some sort of success. But the story of the Special Unit is much more than the flimsy pages of an amateurishly produced magazine, however significant, or good reviews on the arts pages of the broadsheets.

12

A MURDERER, A BAMPOT
AND LIVES TURNED AROUND

To the thousands who followed the emerging story of the Special Unit, as told week after week in the city's tabloids, it was simply sex, drugs, rock and roll behind bars. The deep thinking and the humanity that infected the project is its early years was not headline material. The other stuff was.

The two leading characters in what was almost a prison soap opera were, of course, Jimmy Boyle and Hugh Collins, undoubtedly the most well-known of the Unit's success stories. They were very different people. Boyle's CV is like no other – gangster, murderer, sculptor, novelist, wine buff. Not too many can claim that. Once said to be the most violent man in Scotland, he was jailed in 1967 for the murder of another lowlife gangland figure, William 'Babs' Rooney. He has denied that he committed this killing although not his gangland past. The sentence was life. He immediately became what the prison reports politely call 'difficult to control' and spent long spells in solitary and in the infamous cages of Porterfield, Inverness. He was particularly violent to prison staff and the brutality of the cages did little to calm a tortured soul. The so-called cages, which were reserved for prison troublemakers, were temporarily closed in 1972 after some of the most violent disturbances in a

Scottish prison when five prison officers and four inmates (including Boyle) were hurt.

It seems strange now, looking back on that violent era and the obvious fact that the cages were no solution, that they were reopened and back in use in 1978 before finally being abandoned and demolished in 1994. Ironically, around the same time, the Special Unit was closed. It is a deep source of puzzlement that, as the Special Unit and its basic belief in redemption rather than retribution, crawled slowly to its controversial conclusion, a few miles up the road in the Highlands men were still thrown into the cages that had 'animalized' Boyle.

Hugh Collins is a contrast to Boyle. He is on record at almost every interview he gives of telling of his regret that he took a life. He says his own life was never the same again. Boyle seems less troubled by his crimes and his past, seemingly claiming on occasion that the brutality and pain of his own life of long years of confinement has perhaps blinded him to an earlier and incredibly different way of life. He has attacked those who have publicly grudged him any material success he has had since release by saying: 'The only thing I can say about people like that is that they have allowed themselves to become prisoners of my past. I have moved on but they have allowed themselves to be stuck. My life has moved on beyond my wildest dreams. There is a thrawn jealous aspect to some people's attitude.'

It is a point of view, but to my mind, Hugh Collins' reaction to the Special Unit, and his 'redemption' – and if that word is too strong, 'life change' – is more complex and interesting. The younger man, Collins was jailed in 1975 for the gangland murder of a rival, Willie Mooney. In a laceratingly honest interview on his criminal days and what he had become he said: 'I was never a gangster, only a bampot. The only person I can apologise to is dead. The only man who can forgive me is dead.' The killing of Willie Mooney led to 16 years in jail, long nights awake and in fear. He says: 'I was afraid of death. I was afraid of rejection. I see now how my violence was the product of fear.' That's the sort of mind and thinking ideal for 'treatment' rather than a midnight visit from a 'batter squad' and Collins got it in the Special Unit. Introduced to sculpture, he found some release and peace. His story shows the best side of the Unit and it was played out before the concept of the reformers became contaminated by controversy, drifting discipline and too much outside interference.

Collins, like Boyle, has undoubted talent as a writer and sculptor. One of his most famous pieces, 'Christ, the Sinner', was commissioned by the St Columbus Church in Glasgow but rejected owing to its explicit depiction of Christ's genitalia, though it was subsequently shown in Edinburgh galleries. He tells of the release brought by his new-found skill. Art classes in the Unit gave him sculpting material and access to expert advice: 'I was fortunate. I was no' bad at it. When I had the idea to carve the statue of Christ I took it as a sign. This makes me sound like a maniac. It took me two years, but this is the bizarre thing; it was the best time of my life.' He said he saw the long process of creating a religious work of art as a punishment, a penance. And when he put away the sculptor's chisel and hammer he took to the word processor, producing books like *Autobiography of a Murderer* and *Walking Away*, books full of insight for anyone interested in crime and punishment.

Collins was in many ways the perfect prisoner for the BSU experiment. The regime could have been designed to reform him personally, at least in theory. But Collins was not blind to the faults in an experiment that changed his life and he has been outspoken in his criticism of some aspects of life in the Unit: 'The Special Unit saved me, but it also tortured me. I was made into a pet lion for the social workers, the psychologists and lawyers who came there. Some of it was disgusting. These people were like groupies. They patronised you and got a thrill from being near you. Some of the women who visited the Unit would even sleep with you.'

But it is also revealing that the trust that had been built up by the special breed of prison officers used in the Unit was so strong that men like Boyle and Collins were daily given chisels and hammers and other potentially dangerous weapons. It takes guts to hand a chib merchant a razor-sharp chisel. Indeed a couple of those involved in treating the prisoners tell of the astonishment of such as Boyle and Larry Winters in particular being handed scissors across the table by their captors, chatting face to face. It didn't happen outside the Unit. It was a powerful indicator that inside the Unit you were not treated as an animal, but as a man with brains and potential and some hope for the future. But such an easygoing regime in the centre of a hard prison where even a knife and fork in the dining hall could be a weapon was clearly not acceptable to all. A lot of the opposition to the Unit sprang from hard-line prison officers who had spent years in service and years when handing a prisoner a chisel was invitation to a potentially deadly attack. Their position is, looking back, to a degree understandable. The officers in the Unit were specialists, knowledgeable about the background of the formation of the Unit and basically sympathetic to its aims. Specially selected for the job. Life did not look so simple to the run of the mill officer earning his corn in a mainstream establishment supervising slopping out and restraining hard tickets ready to give him and his colleague a sly kicking at any opportunity.

The newspapers, too, almost from day one, were full of criticism – some of it rumour, some of it fact. Newly released prisoners from the mainstream jail passed the prison scuttlebutt to reporters eager to hear the worst of an experiment that in the end seemed to spiral out of control. Finally the prison authorities simply closed the place down. It might have been a better idea to introduce a firmer hand, cut down on the excesses, persevere and expand the concept and that seemed to be what Alan Bishop of the Prison Inspectorate wanted in 1994. But in the end the authorities folded in the face of relentless public criticism. Noises were made that this was not the end of the ethos of specialized small units for certain types of inmates and indeed that ethos was now to be spread around the country's prisons. But the doors of the BSU were to close for good.

An official report late in the life of the Unit, 'Small units in the Scottish Prison Service', makes fascinating reading. It comments on the problems of the Unit and notes that these came about gradually over the years. But whatever the rights and wrongs of the decision to shut the Unit down, the authors of this report cannot be accused of a whitewash. They stated: 'The near universal view is that in the absence of an active and continuously developing community the BSU has become stagnant and fossilized. Many of the current prisoners have spent lengthy periods of time (in once case ten years) in the Unit often actively refusing to move to another establishment, as this has been seen as a backward move, entailing too many sacrifices. A number of prisoners appear to have "dug in their heels" in the hope of eventually gaining liberation directly from the Unit, or at least a release programme prior to moving on from the Unit. This has, without doubt, led to considerable regime "slippage" to the extent that the regime is currently far more relaxed than was envisaged by the 1971 working party which stated that the Unit should retain "a firm but fair discipline system".' The report then went on to highlight a whole series of practices which it said characterized life in the Unit.

1) Visits have come to dominate virtually the whole of Unit life. There are very few visit-free periods and visitors can often be found in, and arriving at, the Unit when community and special meetings are taking place. While it is important that prisoners are encouraged to re-establish and develop their relationship with their family, and while contact with 'outsiders' can be beneficial and therefore very important, it is inevitable that the current frequency of visits reduces the scope for interaction among prisoners and staff. Indeed, some prisoners have hidden behind a stream of visitors, which has removed the need for them to interact with the Unit community on any regular basis with the result that the community has become less close-knit and less cohesive.

The second note was meat and drink to the critics, officially confirming the worst fears of outside observers on the subject of sex behind bars. It read:

2) In a supposed demonstration of the fact that the Unit ethos is based on the notions of responsibility and trust between staff and prisoners, visits have long been allowed to take place, unsupervised, in prisoners' cells despite the existence of an Operational Instruction to the effect that staff should be present in the cells area when visits are taking place. An additional rule states that cell doors should remain open during visits. In practice, neither of these instructions are enforced on a regular basis and the cells area has virtually become a no-go area for staff with the result that the pris-

oners are effectively, but unofficially, permitted conjugal visits.

Other serious criticisms followed, building up a picture of what the Unit had become that was more powerfully critical than any previous examination of the regime.

3) Prisoners' visitors are not searched on any regular basis or in anything other than a cursory manner. Again this is a practice that has evolved over time and which has supposedly been used as a measure of displaying the level of trust between staff and prisoners. It is difficult to determine whether this trust has been honoured and in the Unit's early days the prisoners were brought to book by the rest of the community if there was any breach of trust by their visitors. It is clear from evidence supplied to the Working Party that breaches of trust have occurred. There have been incidents in the past where both prisoners and their visitors have been found to be under the influence of alcohol and while it is generally claimed that the visitors did their drinking prior to arrival at the Unit there have been incidents when intoxicated visitors have been found in possession of empty spirit bottles on departure from the Unit. There have also been incidents where BSU prisoners have been found in possession of unauthorized substances, indeed, several prisoners have been downgraded as a result of using alcohol whilst in the Unit.

Less sensational but equally telling as an example of how the Unit had, to some extent at least, lost its way was the next observation of the working party. The public perception of the old sex, drugs, rock and roll culture was that it was mitigated by the serious artistic overtones, with the violent men in the Unit spending endless hours in painting, sculpting and producing literature of high quality. In the end it seems that the concept of incarceration and art walking hand in hand was 'out the window' as they say in Glasgow.

4) Only one of the current group of prisoners is regularly engaged in any kind of constructive activity and this is an activity from which he gains significant financial profit. The remainder of the prisoners spend the majority of their time entertaining visitors, reading, watching television or sleeping.

The Working Party document goes on to make many more telling but less headline-grabbing observations. The slow deterioration of group cohesions was illustrated by the fact that very rarely did the final group of prisoners cook or eat together, each prisoner preferring to cook and eat on an individual basis. This was in contrast to what was going on in a Unit in operation at Shotts Prison at the time when prisoners and staff in exceptional and special occasions sat down together to eat. The regime was certainly relaxed and it is easy to see what problems the policy on mail could lead to. In line with prison rules, incoming mail was not censored, but neither were letters opened and checked for contraband in the presence of the prisoners, as is the case in other prisons. A gram here, a gram there and a little help from my friends. . . . The report acknowledged that the 'substantial' regime slippage that allowed such departures from prison norm had taken place slowly over the years. It also observed that with the lengthy periods of time the existing prisoners had spent in the Unit that it 'has been very difficult, and often impossible, for successive staff members or governors to retract "the privileges" which resulted from the "slippage".'

There is no final end to the story of the Special Unit. Arguments about its success or failure and its legacy in the current prison system will continue in the talk on the streets and in more academic circles. Ron Ferguson is one of the names most frequently associated with the great experiment. Cowdenbeath's most famous supporter is now a freelance author, columnist and broadcaster. He was minister of St Magnus Cathedral in Orkney for 11 years and is still based there, and he took time to pen the following account of his own association with the Unit and the conflict it caused even in church circles. He writes:

I first came in contact with the Special Unit in the late 1970s, when I was Church of Scotland community minister in Easterhouse. Community ministry was an experimental form of ministry established by the Kirk; the idea was for a minister to live in a deprived community and work with churches of all denominations, Protestant and Roman Catholic, in ways which would benefit the wider community. Rev Archie Russell (Drumchapel) and myself were the first appointees in 1973.

The street I lived in with my family had its own gang, the Torran Toi, and many of the families in the area had at least one member or relative resident in the 'Big Hoose'. The experience taught me a lot about the circumstances in which violent crime flourishes.

I had been brought up in a mining community in West Fife, but nothing had prepared me for living and working in a community in which male unemployment levels were more than 50 per cent and crime was endemic. I learned at first hand that the herding of people into ghettos, into urban Sowetos, suited society at large. To stick disadvantaged people together into a reservation with few jobs or facilities and then demonise them was an effective distancing tactic, one which permitted a denial of responsibility.

Ordinary people, many of whom had had very abusive child-hoods and who were struggling for survival, became 'evil' in the eyes of those who wanted none of the potential trouble anywhere near their own back yards. I learned about the gulf between 'us' and 'them'. Some people in the Kirk, quite proud of having one of 'us' living among 'them', would ask me: 'Are you winning?' Winning what, precisely? What I knew for sure was that others were losing, drowning even.

Over eight years, I got to know some of the most fright-ening and some of the most fantastic people I have ever met. The experience changed my life.

A remarkable friend of mine, George Wilson, a lay preacher, used to go regularly to the Special Unit at Barlinnie. Set up in 1973, it was the vision of two men, Ken Murray and a civil servant called Alex Stephen. As a prison officer, Murray – a man of gritty integrity, ahead of his time – was concerned that some of Scotland's most violent criminals were simply being banged up without any serious attempt at rehabilitation. Murray and civil servant Stephen were convinced there had to be a better way of dealing with 'uncontrollable' prisoners than chaining them up or sedating them into passivity. The Unit was initially staffed by volunteer prison officers and run on democratic lines, with prisoners allowed a voice and a vote. The lifers were given access to teachers and art materials, and encouraged to express themselves without violence.

George Wilson was one of the volunteers. He was teaching a man serving a life sentence for murder how to look after budgies. It seemed bizarre to me. It gave 'I'd like to wring her neck' a new meaning. But no necks were wrung. The violent lifer learned how to care tenderly for budgies. And became more human in the process. George felt that I should visit. The only problem was that the Special Unit had been declared – by a vote of inmates and staff – a clergy-free zone. George spoke to them persuasively, and they voted. So I became the first minister to darken the doors of the Special Unit.

I got to know the infamous James Boyle. Under the old prison regime, Boyle had attacked prison warders, and covered the walls of his cell with his own excrement. But now that he was being treated as a human being instead of a piece of shit himself, he was making sculpture. The man had a talent. He made beautiful and expressive things. I learned about his background. What would I have become, if I had had his upbringing? I had no answer to that question.

Nothing could excuse his crimes. He had been a really hard man, working for loan sharks in the Gorbals. But was he pure evil, the monster the tabloids talked about?

The red tops screamed against the Special Unit. When Boyle was allowed out to attend one of his own exhibitions, people went crazy.

What I discovered was that there were powerful people who wanted him to fail, in order to prove their own theories that the likes of Boyle *couldn't* change. One former Moderator was vehement in his view that the Special Unit should be shut down forthwith. There were church people who – and I choose my words carefully – *wanted* Boyle to re-offend.

The sight of a notoriously violent man changing was, strangely, too much for some clerics. His redemption wasn't according to church formulae. He didn't grovel enough, didn't show enough self-loathing, didn't use the right coded language. *Somehow a changed, articulate Boyle was more of a threat than one who lived like a caged animal.*

The rage became even worse when Boyle wrote about his experiences. Then when another lifer, Larry Winters, made a powerful sculpture of a naked Christ, the anger was truly murderous. Christ was the property of the Church, not of evil murderers! And despite the biblical accounts of the crucifixion, the Word-became-flesh was acceptable only if it was androgynous, sanitised and wearing first-century Palestinian Y-fronts.

I cannot justify the crimes of the Special Unit's inmates; but nor could I justify the creation of urban ghettos, and the monsterising and scapegoating of people. I regard people like Ken Murray and Alex Stephen as heroes, as was Geoff Shaw, convener of Strathclyde Regional Council, who befriended some fairly desperate people and argued for prison reform. When I told Boyle I was writing Shaw's biography, Boyle said: 'Geoff had a magic about him. He always made you feel, you're important to me. He always left you feeling good. He challenged everything you thought you knew about churchmen. We were all conditioned to accepting the Protestant/Catholic thing, but he challenged all that. He made you think.

'Hardened prisoners aren't good at expressing emotion. They would say, "Geoff Shaw, he's no' a bad c***." That spoke volumes. He presented tenderness and love and all the things we were repressing. All the prisoners I knew respected him.'

The Special Unit closed in 1995 – too expensive, apparently. The work of rehabilitation is costly, but it is cheap at the price. Ken Murray, who had gone on to chair the social work committee of Strathclyde Regional Council, resigned his 50-year membership of the Labour party, accusing the Labour leadership of sacrificing principles to gain power.

The scales of justice are still tilted in favour of the rich and the powerful; it is not so much the good as the poor who die

young in today's Scotland. And I am also grateful to some
desperate people, in Easterhouse and in Barlinnie, who taught
me more than theologians about the meaning of that most
precious word, redemption.'

You can't get a more elegant and perceptive summary of the
Special Unit than that.

13

AT WAR IN THE BAR-L
ON LAND AND SEA

During the two great world wars of the last century life went on mostly as usual in Barlinnie, and the newspaper headlines featuring the largest prison in Scotland were overshadowed by news from the war zones and the latest casualty figures from the various fronts. But men of the people like the Independent Labour Party's firebrand Jimmy Maxton still had an interest in what was going on in the prison on his constituency doorstep. Maxton, who died in 1946 and for years represented Glasgow Bridgeton, had some inside knowledge of prisons having spent a year incarcerated for campaigning against the First World War. He was a conscientious objector and given work on barges.

He was considered one of the greatest orators of his time and his questions to Parliament were carefully thought out and not without the occasional sarcastic observation, as on the occasion in March 1940 when he asked the then Secretary of State for Scotland 'whether he is aware that part of Barlinnie Prison, Glasgow, is being used as a military prison; whether the prisoners in it are segregated from the ordinary civilian prisoners; and whether the military prisoners are under the control of the prison governor and the regular prison warders, or entirely under military control?' One would have assumed that the

Secretary of State would have been well aware of what was going on. In the event David Colville did not rise to the bait and contented himself by simply saying, 'The answer to the first two parts of the question is in the affirmative. As regards the last part the military prisoners are entirely under military control.'

The socialist persisted.

Mr Maxton: Is the ordinary civilian governor in control of the whole prison and both civilian and military prisoners?

Mr Colville: No, sir, a part of the prison has been handed over to the military authorities.

The debate continued with Davie Kirkwood, a former ILP colleague of Maxton and with a similar firebrand CV as a left-winger and political stirrer, chipping in with a question delivered with, one would surmise, his tongue firmly in his cheek:

Mr Kirkwood: Do I understand that there is plenty of room in Barlinnie for other individuals? I was informed that the Duke Street prison in Glasgow could not be demolished as there was no other place available in which to put prisoners, and now it seems that there is plenty of room in Barlinnie Prison, which was said to be overcrowded, to accommodate soldier prisoners.

Mr Colville: That is another matter.

This vignette shows prisons as a political football, even in the midst of war, and Barlinnie overcrowding which would still be causing anger nearly 70 years later. You wonder what humanitarians like Maxton and Kirkwood would have made of the large numbers languishing two to a tiny cell in the twenty-first century.

Barlinnie in the First World War, too, played a significant role in the story of Scotland. Respected historian, author and *Sunday*

Herald columnist Trevor Royle published a remarkable book in 2006 – *Flowers of the Forest: Scotland And The First World War* – which chronicled the militant activism around at the time of the conflict and how many objectors to the war ended up in the Bar-L. These were intellectual prisoners and protestors of a very different stripe from the violent men plucked from the city streets and sentenced to do time. In it he details the many street demonstrations and the strong feelings of the men who went to prison rather than fight in the armed forces. Glasgow women – always a strong-minded lot – also organized rent strikes. According to Royle, out of all this, including the activities of men like Tom Bell, John Wheatley and John Maclean, the legend of the Red Clydeside was burnished.

Workers' leaders in these turbulent times faced the constant threat of arrest and trial, among them Maxton, John Muir, and Willie Gallacher. Others were banished in internal exile to Edinburgh. Maclean was dealt with most harshly. Several jail terms were handed down to him, the last in Barlinnie. Maclean was a convinced and consistent campaigner against the slaughter of the First World War. He held hugely well-attended rallies in Bath Street and at the fountain at Shawlands Cross. Maclean had a large army of followers, pacifists and anti-war protestors. At one time they held regular meetings in the old Metropole theatre in Stockwell Street on Sunday nights. But as the war progressed and the newspapers filled with reports of British deaths, a backswell of patriotism grew to oppose them and the rallies tended to move away from the spotlight of the city centre to local halls.

It was brave in these times to speak out in public as Maclean did: 'I have been enlisted in the socialist army for 15 years. God damn all other armies. Any soldier who shoots another soldier in the war is a murderer.' His early arrests came under that handy catch-all for the police, breach of the peace. But Maclean's stance against the war was much more serious than that. And in the end it was the Defence of the Realm Act that sent him on his way to jail. The case against him was that his outspoken public speaking on the morality of war was likely to harm the war effort and prejudice recruiting. The legal moves against him began with a few fines and escalated. He also was fired as a teacher by Govan School Board. The balloon finally burst in 1916 when he was arrested on his way to his home in Pollokshaws after a rally in Bath Street. He was taken to the Central police station en route to Edinburgh Castle where he was held as a prisoner of war and given a choice of a court martial or appearing before the high court. He went for a day in court and was convicted of four of six charges laid against him.

This was no surprise to the firebrand, but the sentence was: three years. He was treated harshly. The first month was spent in the capital's old Calton Jail, where the food was vile and the staff, some recruited from the army and mental institutions, were cruel. The regime was similar to that in some other Scottish prisons at the time: solitary confinement in a cell with no mattress for the first 60 days, no reading matter, no talking to inmates or wardens, one letter, one visit every three months. Convict 2652 was silenced, out of the loop in the anti-war campaigning. But he was far from forgotten. One rally in Glasgow Green, attended by around 100,000, demanded his release. The Glaswegians once again showed their characteristic independence and that, no matter their own patriotic feelings, they also respected John Maclean and his sincerity.

After a time he was sent to Peterhead where he damaged his health with a hunger strike after a request to be moved to Barlinnie was turned down. He was force-fed in a degrading manner. He was also making accusations that his food had been drugged. He was still a celebrated figure in British politics and there was even a protest meeting in London's Albert Hall calling for him to be released. The end of the war on 11 November 1918 was the catalyst for his release. He stood as a Republican candidate for the Gorbals seat aged barely 40, but by now his travails had made him look twice that age. The public was still not ready for his brand of revolution and he got only a few thousand votes.

The authorities were still suspicious of the firebrand and his street corner meetings were spied on. After one such event in Airdrie he was back in custody for using language 'calculated and likely to cause sedition and disaffection among His Majesty's Forces and among the civil population'. This time his destination was Barlinnie and the authorities were wise enough not to court unrest by force-feeding such a political celebrity, even if he was a long-time thorn in their flesh. Instead, he was granted the unique status of a political prisoner, allowed to wear his own clothes, eat his own food and have his own books – and there were no hunger strikes. He was soon released but then rearrested shortly after for egging on the starving unemployed in the Gorbals to direct action. This time it was for a year and he left Barlinnie for the last time in October 1922.

He died the next year and thousands lined the streets for the funeral procession. His legacy has spawned many books, poems and songs. In one poem Hugh MacDiarmid wrote that 'of all Maclean's foes not one was his peer' and described him in another as 'both beautiful and red'. No argument he was one of the most intellectual of men to do time in the Bar-L. I wonder how many of the current inmates are aware of him and his connection with their current place of incarceration. Perhaps more than you might expect.

*   *   *

All this activity by Maclean and others had a lasting effect in the political life of Scotland, sometimes sowing the seed of the demand for independence. But it does seem remarkable that the prison experiences of such intellectuals did not result in long-term changes in the most inhumane parts of penal policy like shared cells and slopping out. Especially if you consider that at one time, much later than the Red Clydeside era, it has to be said, there were so many Labour politicians doing time that it was half joked the prison name should be changed from Barlinnie to 'Baillies'ton in deference to the political nature of some of the inmates. Joking aside you would have thought that the jailing of many politicians, conscientious objectors and others, would have led to more of a public clamour to ameliorate the conditions in which prisoners were held. But it did not seem to happen. Noise there may have been but little action in the jails.

Apart from the Red Clydesiders, another political activist to taste porridge in Barlinnie was a Londoner called Guy Aldred – for a lifelong revolutionary the name Guy was apt, though it had come about by the mundane fact that he was born on Guy Fawkes Day 1886. Aldred, an anarchist and pioneer communist, got into all sorts of scrapes with the law in London before coming north, attracted some say by the citizens' infamously truculent attitude, rebellious spirit and disrespect for leaders. Just the place for an anarchist to set up camp. He was to end up doing jail time in his adopted city, but he first tasted imprisonment in the south when he waged a constant battle to resist joining the armed forces during the First World War. He was jailed in Winchester, but in August 1916 he was sent to Aberdeenshire to Dyce work camp. This is a long forgotten horror. Prisoners were held in rudimentary conditions in tents in a granite quarry where the ground was a sea of mud. There were other similar places around Britain and the remarkable figure of 69 conscientious objectors died in them.

Guy Aldred, as you would expect of a man with his political views, simply walked out of Dyce, but was soon rearrested in England. It is illustrative of penal conditions at the time to read of his treatment. His constant protesting to the authorities when imprisoned at a Military Camp led to a court martial, his third and not his last, and he was sent to Wandsworth Prison where he was judged to be a ringleader in a planned 'work and discipline strike' by the prisoners. He along with some of his co-conspirators was sentenced to 'No.1 Punishment'. This consisted of 42 days solitary confinement with three days on bread and water and then three days off, locked in a bare unheated basement cell. When this was over, Aldred and his friends were sent to Brixton. Throughout his various confinements Aldred somehow managed to smuggle out articles to be printed in the anarchist press. So it seems that even in such tough days in tough prisons security was not all that effective! Though now the smuggling is mostly in the other direction and the contraband is drugs. At the end of the war Aldred's new life in Glasgow began. He got a huge welcome and spoke at a meeting organized by the Glasgow Anarchists, but on a trip back south he was rearrested and again sent to Wandsworth.

Back in Glasgow in 1921, the constant agitation continued and an article by Guy Aldred appeared in a paper called *The Red Commune* advocating the Sinn Fein tactic of standing for election, but not taking the oath or your seat. This landed him back in the dock. Along with anarchist/communist colleagues he was charged with 'exciting popular disaffection, commotion, and violence to popular authority'. It must have been one of the rarest of charges to get someone a ticket to the Bar-L. Guy Aldred was sentenced at a trial in the Glasgow High Court to a year in Barlinnie and served the full time plus four months on remand. This harsh sentence made some prison history – it was the first time the authorities had said that the months on remand did not count as part of his year's sentence. A female colleague, Jane Patrick, was sent to Duke Street Prison. Guy Aldred lived until 1963 and became a well-kent figure, propagandising until his death. Some credit him as a one-man forerunner of the Citizen's Advice Bureau. He dispensed free advice to all and sundry who came to him for help. For 60 years – except for his time in prisons – he spoke every May Day at a rally. His politics verged on the extreme, but his life of struggle and his consistency earned the affection, if sometimes a tad begrudging, of his fellow Glaswegians.

In Barlinnie in the Second World War for his 'idealism', Aldred shared his time with men with no social conscience, men with no conscience at all, violent men with no instinctive bond with their fellows. A little anecdote told in the wartime diary of a Gordon Highlander shows how tough these guys were. There was a mini riot in the military wing with prisoners smashing up the dining hall and the army decided that the best place for 25 of these troublemakers was not the Bar-L but Taunton military prison, which, although set in beautiful countryside, was reputed to be the toughest establishment in the military.

A handful of Gordon Highlanders was dispatched to the Scottish prison and issued with the handles of spades normally used to dig trenches. These pickaxe-style weapons were to provide protection against the hard men who were to be escorted south. They came in handy. The 20 or so prison troublemakers selected were pushed on to a bus and driven to Central Station where a special carriage, attached to the London train, awaited them. Prisoners and soldiers were met by a mob in the station, but with police help the soldiers managed to get the prisoners through to the carriage. In the general melee one prisoner managed to leg it through the mob of passengers, police and soldiers to nearby Gordon Street, but was swiftly caught. When he arrived back at the train he was said by the army men to 'look a bit roughed up'. Probably something of an understatement.

The journey was barely an hour old when carriage windows were broken and shards of broken glass used to threaten the escorts. The spade handles soon proved their worth and this little mutiny was subdued. Next came a stop in a tunnel near Birmingham and this time a handful of prisoners took off into the darkness and escaped. The journey to Taunton took ten hours and the special carriage with the Barlinnie contingent was shunted from train to train. On arrival at the military prison the reluctant passengers were now much quieter, tired by the long journey and fearful of what would become of them in this tough jail. They were apparently helped on the way into their new home by the boots of the large number of Red Caps who had assembled to welcome them.

The Second World War also saw political prisoners cool their heels in Barlinnie, wrapped in the beliefs that prevented them joining the fighting forces. These idealists didn't just fight against conscription; they were also against such routine matters as air raid precautions and compulsory fire watching schemes. One of the most prominent dissidents was Frank Leech, an anarchist who, before the war, had given shelter to a number of fellow anarchists belonging to a German group who advocated the assassination of Hitler. He also ran a radical bookshop in Buchanan Street in Glasgow which was associated with the Anti-Parliamentary Communist Federation.

At a time when the ordinary citizen was dining on bread and marge and maybe an egg or so a week and carefully going around the house switching off lights and covering windows with blackout paper to make life difficult for the German bomber pilots, anarchists like Leech and Eddie Fenwick were ferociously fighting against such mundane day-to-day parts of the war effort. Fenwick justified refusing to fire watch by saying since 'owners of private property had denied him the elementary rights of man, he was entitled to refuse to protect private property'. Leech was of similar opinion and was fined for refusing to comply with the fire watching regulations. He refused to pay and was sent to Barlinnie where, in the tradition of political prisoners, he promptly went on hunger strike. He went without food for 17 days and was eventually released when friends paid his fine.

The strength of anti-war feeling was extremely strong in conscientious objectors and sometimes it started young. One young Queen's Park secondary school boy was, for example, sent home for refusing to carry a gas mask. He went on to be a well-known conscientious objector.

Leech's threat not to submit to the authorities as long as he had a breath left in him was not empty posturing. He could well have starved himself to death. Hunger strikes, of course, are common in prisons and such as TC Campbell, wrongly imprisoned for the Doyle murders in the Ice Cream wars, often resorted to them. But only occasionally do they result in death.

Barlinnie in the Hitler war was often busy with conscientious objectors. Another notable anti-war protestor was Philip Boyle, a young civil service student who was a most reluctant private in the Highland Light Infantry. He was court-martialled in May 1940 for disobeying a lawful command while on active service. He had refused to wear his military uniform. 'No one is going to make me a soldier' was the stance of the young man from Todd Street, Dennistoun, who was the first Catholic conscientious objector to face court martial in Britain.

The Catholic hierarchy of the time and the Catholic press argued that a Catholic could not be an objector but Boyle was sent to Barlinnie military prison by way of Maryhill Barracks. He seems to have suffered some rough handling by the military. When his father visited him in prison he found him clad only in an old mackintosh and the army uniform which had been forced on him lay on the floor. On his release from this sentence he was again court-martialled for a not wearing a uniform. This time he was sent down to Barlinnie civil prison for 98 days.

The *Scottish Daily Express* reported his case in an interesting fashion. Boyle appeared in court in his own brown suit and Gordon Stott, Advocate, said: 'It shows that in the eyes of the military authorities he had proved his case.' Boyle was asked if, as a non-combatant, he would do farm work and he answered, 'Nothing I am compelled to do.' This prompted Mr Stott to make a remarkable comment on life in the civilian section of wartime Barlinnie. He said: 'Boyle seems to be going to the limit. I have seen his cell and I think that anyone who is prepared to put up with such conditions is a very strong objector.' Eventually this determined young man was granted conditional exemption from army service and directed to work on land drainage, forestry or agriculture. He had endured a lot to make his point.

Stott's comment on conditions in the prison were echoed the following year, in 1941, in the Commons when Willie Gallacher asked the Secretary of State for War 'whether he is aware that visitors to Barlinnie detention camp have to speak to the detained soldiers through iron bars; that the soldiers are in small cubicles three feet away; that as many as four visits may take place at a time with visitors and soldiers trying to make themselves understood above each others' voices; and can modern methods be introduced instead of this method of dealing with visitors?'

Viscount Margesson replied, 'I am aware that the facilities for interview at the military prison and detention barracks to which my Honorable friend refers have been unsatisfactory and the construction of alternative accommodation has been put in hand some time ago. I am glad to say the new premises have now been completed and are already in use.' Willie Gallacher was a wee bit dubious about this answer and continued: 'Are we to understand that this method of receiving visitors will be stopped? It is only two weeks since I was there visiting and I had this experience.' The Secretary of State for War told him he hoped the new arrangements would be satisfactory. It is curiously reassuring that in the darkest days of war, with cities under attack from the Nazi bombers and soldiers fighting desperate battles on the front line, that Red Clydesiders and Viscounts alike were still able to keep a civilised eye on what was going on in the Bar-L.

Around the same time that the rash of conscientious objectors were serving time in the early forties, Barlinnie had another high-profile political inmate, Arthur Donaldson, who was the leader of the SNP from 1960 to 1969. Dundee is famed for jute, jam and journalism and as 'furry boots city', as the Glaswegians call it, was Donaldson's hometown, it was no surprise that a political thinker and future party leader would try his hand at the newspaper trade there. Later he went to America to try to further a career in journalism but ended up in the motor industry in Detroit. He joined the SNP as an overseas member in 1928 but returned to Scotland in 1936 to work in farming. But he made some unwanted headlines when in May 1941 his home was raided by the police who suspected him and a number of other SNP figures of 'subversive activity' due to their support for the Scottish Neutrality League, naturally an organisation not much favoured by the authorities in the dark days of the early forties. Donaldson was arrested and interned under Defence Regulation 18B firstly in Kilmarnock Prison and latterly in Barlinnie. He was held for six weeks and released without charge.

At the time his arrest was explained by his opposition against the conscription of Scottish women to be taken to work in English factories for the war effort. Some former colleagues felt this made him a political prisoner. But in November 2005 a MI5 file was released suggesting he was a German sympathiser. Even before this, in 1994, such accusations had been made and absolutely denied by his widow Vi and the leaders of the SNP at the time. No evidence for the allegations has ever been produced. Donaldson died in 1993.

One of the most intriguing tales to emerge from wartime Barlinnie involved no politicians or army prisoners at all. It is featured in *The Jail That Went to Sea* by Peter Haining. Unlikely as it seems, the Bar-L became involved in what might be called a modern press gang. Again the year was 1941 and Britain was in trouble on the high seas, suffering losses of merchant ships equivalent to seven million tons a year. It is said they were being sunk at three times the rate we could build new ones. The Americans agreed to help out by building new vessels under the Lend-Lease agreement. But they wanted the ships crewed by Brits and at this time in the war manpower losses were mounting. Someone somewhere had the idea of a return to the press gang era and the government surreptitiously began scouring the jails for ex-cons to convert into seamen.

Five of Bridgeton's hardest left their Barlinnie cells in August 1941 and were somehow or other convinced that they should join a Lend-Lease ship, the *George Washington*. It is not explained if they were sandbagged or drugged to be woken up at sea in traditional press gang style. But these guys did join the ship. Their merchant service only lasted a few weeks and the action they got involved in was not dodging U-boats or shooting down Nazi planes. The Glasgow hard men lived the legend and created mayhem ashore in Halifax, Nova Scotia, Montreal and New York. Two jumped ship at the first opportunity and the other three had to be banned from the boiler room of the ship taking them back to the UK after causing all sorts of bother. They even planned a mutiny with the idea of taking the vessel to South America. But the skipper, with aid from some tough regular stokers, almost literally hit that one on the head. After the ship was handed back to the Americans the other three also disappeared.

These days the denizens of gangland Glasgow milk social services for every penny they can get while simultaneously milking their fellow citizens of their hard-earned cash. The Barlinnie Crew of 70 years or so ago were ahead of their time – while they inflicted mayhem on their shipmates and innocent punters in the waterfront bars of the east coast of America they were on full pay from the government!

14

THE ELECTRIC CHAIR
AND PLUGGING IN TO HISTORY

As Barlinnie, in the early years of the twenty-first century, struggles to cope with the twin tasks of imprisoning and reha- bilitating growing numbers of offenders, two problems are depressingly familiar – overcrowding and the misuse of drugs. Neither problem is likely to go away soon. Only knocking down the Victorian jail and building a massive new prison in the Glasgow area will have any real effect on overcrowding in the penal system in the west of Scotland. Drugs on the streets, in the cells, or as dispensed by the prison health centre will likewise be with us well into the foreseeable future. But there can be a little more short-term optimism on the drugs front. Quite how to reduce the massive prescribing of methadone inside the prison is not clear. But dealing with drugs smuggled into the jail can, hopefully, be tackled by staff determination and the help of new technology.

In 2011, hi-tech solutions are in use in a new drive on secu- rity in the prison. The new technology works alongside that old stand-by, the sniffer dog. The canine ability to sniff out mind-altering substances should not be underestimated. And, of course, there is still the fall back of physical searches of the body orifices of newly admitted prisoners, and sometimes visitors, suspected of smuggling. Human ingenuity is immense when it comes to getting drugs past all forms of security and into the hands of men desperate for something to release their minds from the boredom and depression of incarceration. Chocolate eggs intended to be sold as a wee treat to children can turn up stuffed with drugs and nastily hidden in a new inmate's body. Unpleasant work for officers. The latest security drive is using the hi-tech methods. 'Electric chairs' have been bought in a move to stop cons smuggling mobile phones, sim cards, knives or drugs into the jail hidden in body orifices. The new machines are used in tandem with other sensitive drug tracing devices and, of course, those sniffer dogs. The new chairs were an innovation first used in the States where they have been successful and the hope is that the investment of £100,000 on these and other hi-tech gadgets will stop the smuggling of all sorts of items into prisons.

On admission, inmates now have to sit on the Body Orifice Security Scanner ('BOSS' – a nice touch!). If anything suspicious is detected there is a bleeping noise and red alerts flash. The chair itself looks like a hi-tech version of 'Old Sparky', the favourite method of dispatching gangsters in movies and sadly still in use in the States today. Sitting in it might just give even a hard ticket a frisson of fear. These new scanning machines can be used routinely, not just in cases where there is real suspicion that a distressing – to inmate and prison officer alike – search of body orifices is necessary. Each individual 'electric chair' costing £6,500 is sensitive enough to detect metal items as small as a pin or a drug needle. The prison service says: 'We have bought nine BOSS chairs and have one in every prison including two in Barlinnie. We have also spent £40,000 on mobile drug tracing machines. These are all measures brought in to improve security at jails.'

Drugs and mobile phones are two of the biggest current prison problems. No figures yet exist on the success of BOSS in the Bar-L, but the size of the problem can be illustrated by the fact that in 2008 one scanner found 28 mobiles phones inside Dublin's Cloverhill Prison. Phones, of course, are vital for those who like to rule their old gangs or set up new scams from behind bars. And there are more of these guys around than you might expect. BOSS may look like a reject from a *Star Trek* set but it is clearly a much needed new armament for officers in the front line of the drugs war.

All this is a good example of the thinking on the way ahead for the penal system that is going on in Barlinnie and elsewhere. In his nine years in the job, the ex-Governor, Bill McKinlay and his staff have made great strides in civilising the prison. The atmosphere in the halls and in the workshops is far removed from that which pertained at the time of the rooftop protests in the eighties or indeed in what they called the 'tobacco riots' of the thirties.

In the departed days of the Special Unit there was much talk of trust between officers and prisoners. That trust is clearly evident today, particularly in the woodworking areas where cons and officers work together in an environment which, with hammers, chisels and other tools, has real potential for danger.

Walk the prison with ex-Governor McKinlay or his senior lieutenants and you immediately sense a feeling of respect for the staff from the majority of the prisoners. That said, there's no doubt that there will always be, in any prison, some incorrigible and basically unreformable men at odds with any form of authority. There will also be those bitter men who still protest their innocence. And the history of crime in this city does show that there have been many horrific examples of wrongful imprisonment, from Oscar Slater to the Ice Cream wars.

Bill McKinlay is a friendly, humane man, a man with vast experience of the prison service – and dealing with the press. He answers questions crisply and in a no-nonsense way. Before being appointed governor he had only been in the prison on two occasions, once to enter the charity run round the internal perimeter and the other to help manage the major incident in '87. On starting the Barlinnie job, his initial reaction included the thought that it was outdated in that you got soaked walking the uncovered areas between the five great halls, the educational set-up and the workshops. He is open and friendly and all the usual old chestnut questions posed at a governor are handled without flannel. Before his retirement we had an interesting little question and answer session.

Q. What is the realistic chance of escaping from Barlinnie?

A. The Scottish Prison Service's historical record is very good, the annual performance is a success story. I would like to think it is very difficult to escape. Even if that is achieved, where could anyone go as this country is an island and now has agreement with many other countries to repatriate such people should they try for a 'safe' haven.

Q. Are conditions suitable for families visiting or would you change them?

A. Conditions are suitable but I would like more time available. Visits can be a heavy demand on families. Years ago prisoners would save from what little earnings they got to send money out; now it is the other way round.

Q. Are you irritated by the outside conception of some that prison life is cushy?

A. Not irritated, but saddened by a media-driven created perception that is far from reality.

Q. What is the situation on firearms, riot shields etc for officers?

A. There are no firearms or the intention to have such. We have Personal Protective Equipment for all aspects of the prison, from catering to removal teams.

Q. How horrific is the prison experience for white-collar criminals?

A. The experience affects everyone in different ways no matter the type of offence. It is not a normal situation and to be deprived of one's freedom must have an impact on all who experience it – no matter what they say.

Q. Are current procedures for training officers suitable for penal operations in the twenty-first century?

A. Yes.

Q. What are your thoughts on open prisons?

A. All prisoners, if time permits, should go through an incremental process of gradual freedom back into the community so the open prison concept is a necessary and a good one.

Q. What is the situation with smoking in the prison?

A. Smoking is not allowed by staff or prisoners on SPS property. There is one exception to this as a cell, for the purpose of legislation, is designated as the prisoner's residence and he can smoke in it.

Q. What is the way ahead for Barlinnie and the prison service in Scotland?

A. Physical redevelopment, i.e. new builds. The way the prisoner population projections are going it will need an expansion programme to deal with the demand. Alternatives need to be used and accepted or we will face a significant cost to the public purse that we cannot afford.

Q. What is the prime piece of advice you would give to your successor?

A. Do not stand still and keep delivering initiatives even in the face of high prison numbers and overcrowding. Such pressures make it all the more important that good service and the delivery of same is maintained, not used as an excuse for not improving or moving on.

Two, more personal, questions provided interesting answers.

Bill McKinlay was part of the face of the constant struggle to serve both prisoners and society in Barlinnie. His new deputy, appointed in summer 2009, is part of a changing future for the prison service. Rhona Hotchkiss is making history in the Scottish Prison Service, one of three people recently recruited from outside the service to step into the job at the high level of deputy governor. With a background in the top levels of the NHS, she saw an advert for the job. The challenge of being an 'outsider' recruited to take a position at the very top of the penal hierarchy appealed to her. It was a bold move by the prison service to recruit successful people from the outside who would have the ability to look at what was going on in prisons, and help run them, by seeing the whole organisation in a different way from others who had come up through the system.

Rhona's academic background ticked all the right boxes – an honours degree in religion and philosophy from the Open University, an organisation for which she has the highest praise. Her experience, too, in nursing was also valuable. Indeed it is becoming more evident that prison officers are concerned with much, much more than security – their training puts great emphasis on the need to work to rehabilitate their charges and consider what happens to them when the happy day of release eventually arrives and the doors close behind them. All this is a trend that should be much refreshed by the introduction of people like Rhona Hotchkiss. Incidentally, the other two recently recruited newcomers at deputy governor level came from top jobs in banking and private industry.

It seems a tough job for a woman, though the prison service has had a succession of top female executives, starting from Lady Martha Bruce, through the legendary Agnes Curran of Dungavel, to the present day Director of Prisons, Rona Sweeney. Rhona Hotchkiss is not phased by some of the rough aspects of the job. Like Agnes Curran, Rhona finds that even the toughest of prisoners tend in general to show respect to a female and even if given a mouthful by some character or another it is no new experience. You can get that, too, in the front line of the health service. And a female face about the place can bring a sense of normality and balance to what is otherwise an alien environment.

Rhona has thought deeply about the way forward for the prison service and one of the things she is unhappy about in the current system is short sentences: 'They don't work. They leave us no time to engage with prisoners in looking at their offending behaviour or the factors that lead to it; they cost a lot of money and for very little return for the public. I'd support any attempt to find alternatives to prison that are sustainable and more likely to reduce re-offending. The argument about getting rid of short sentences being a way of letting dangerous criminals loose on the streets just doesn't wash. If they're that dangerous, why are they only being sent to prison for seven days or a month in the first place?'

There is no getting away from the point made by Governor McKinlay time and time again in newspaper and television interviews – Barlinnie has reached the end of its useful life. It must be knocked down and replaced. But maybe even that will provide an unlikely opportunity for Glasgow to winkle some real long-term good out of this grim place. Odd as it seems to some, prison museums and 'experiences' can be a potent tourist attraction. There is a successful example just a few miles away from the Bar-L in Inveraray Jail, which is now an outstanding tourist attraction in Argyll.

The idea of the Bar-L as a museum reminds me of a visit to Alcatraz, which is now a huge San Francisco tourist attraction. You get there by launch, setting out from Pier 33 near Fishermen's Wharf, and it's a pleasant sail across San Francisco Bay. A crab sandwich and a cold beer make the journey all the more memorable. And for the tourists it is a round trip as the Americans say, unlike the sail across the bay for the wiseguys and bad guys heading for the island 'Pen'. However it has to be said that it's a bit more glamorous than taking the bus to Riddrie. On the way across there is plenty of time to see the expanse of the bay that made the island such a fortress. It is said no one ever escaped alive from the penitentiary during its 29 years of operation. More than 30 inmates were involved in 14 escape plots. Twenty-three were recaptured, six were shot and killed fleeing from the authorities and two drowned.

Prison humour is worldwide and Alcatraz has its fair share. A tourist rubbernecking round the pen is shown Broadway (the main thoroughfare lined with cells). The guide who showed round the group I was in was an ex-inmate. What had caged him on the island was not dwelt on, but by now he was an old guy reliving his time in the cells alongside such as Big Al (Capone's own cell is a major exhibit) and other big-time criminals. The old guy could wring the last ounce of emotion out of the hundreds of tourists who go to the island each day. His real tearjerker was the story of Hogmanay on Alcatraz, 'New Years' as he called it. Locked in the cells the inmates could hear the sound of the festivities drifting across the moonlit waters of the bay, 'Old Lang Syne', the fireworks. You could almost hear the clink of the bottles and the pop of the corks, he said. That night, like no other, you knew you were locked away on the outside of society.

A visit to the former home of birdman Robert Stroud and guys like bank robber Thomas Limerick help make for a good day out – even the kids seem to enjoy it. In this *Barlinnie Story* we have dealt with some pretty violent episodes, but not one quite as bloody as the death of bank robber Thomas Limerick. He was one of Alcatraz's would-be escapers. Along with a couple of other cons, he used a hammer from the furniture workshop to club a warder to death and then stormed the gun tower on top of the building. The guard there shot Limerick, injured one of his co-conspirators and the third was captured. Who says prison museums are not fascinating? It is interesting that Alcatraz is both on the US register of Historic Places and is designated a US National Historic Landmark.

No doubt many of the Barlinnie governors had their nick-names, most unprintable but, as far as I can see, none that featured in the public prints. But Alcatraz prisoners did a colourful side-line in nicknaming their governors. The first was James A Johnston and he wanted only America's most incorrigible and most unman-ageable prisoners delivered to his care. He was called 'Saltwater' because of his practice of hosing down unruly inmates. Edwin Swope was 'Cowboy' because of his Stetsons, and Paul Madigan was 'Promising Paul' so called because he was a good listener to the problems of inmates, but nothing much ever happened!

Other examples of tourism and prisons include Tombstone in Arizona, of Boot Hill and the Gunfight at the OK Corral fame. The courthouse and jail here were the backdrop to the exploits of Wyatt Earp and the Clanton and McLaury brothers. The gallows still stands in the court precincts. There are other examples of prisons as a tourist draw, like Old Melbourne jail and its Ned Kelly connections.

A little imagination could be of use here. In my view when the long-awaited demolition of the Bar-L happens, one of the great halls should be left standing as a Museum of Criminal Justice. The tall chimneys and great walls would still be a dominant feature of the east end skyline. Keep the cells, as they were, keep the echoing landings and staircases. Display the menus and how they changed down the years, and chart the changing regimes showing how they gradually became more civilised. Recreate a touch of the horror of slopping out with a display of chamber pots and remind visitors of the reality of death at the end of a rope with photographs of the death cell and gallows. There would be no shortage of exhibits. But add some extra value to a visit down prison memory lane by relocating the police Black Museum from its city centre Pitt Street HQ to the lone surviving hall. The police service's own museum, currently near Glasgow Cross, could also be moved to the east end to add to the experience.

And a final thought. A large area in this new attraction, a prison museum like no other, could be given over to record the turbulent years of the Barlinnie Special Unit. And to house a collection of the remarkable works of art, creative writing, drawing, painting and sculpture created by the singular men, murderers who had their lives changed forever, men who found redemption inside the walls of Barlinnie. Now that would be a place worth travelling to from any part of the world to visit.

Bill McKinlay listened to the clang of Barlinnie's doors for a final time when he headed into a well-deserved retirement in Autumn 2010. His successor, Derek McGill is a prison service veteran with vast experience garnered over 30 years in all sorts of establishments. Derek is a savvy guy with a friendly air of authority, a man who has seen both good and bad in his long years. He loves his job, much heartened by any successes that see cons walk out and go straight. But realistic about the failures. He is not out of sympathy with the museum idea but has priorities more important than my perhaps fanciful notion of building a new prison and turning Barlinnie into an unlikely tourist attraction. Talking to him it is obvious that it would take a lot to shake him, clearly a good man to have at your side in the trenches as well as a forward thinking manager. One of his particular interests is 'incident management' and I got the feeling that any cons thinking of trouble – be it a wee dining hall rammy or maybe a full scale riot like those of the eighties and thirties in the Bar-L – would do well to realise they would have to deal with a determined man who has made a deep study of prison unrest and how to deal with it. That said it should also be pointed out that within the prison community Derek enjoys a reputation as 'very fair'. Before the Barlinnie appointment he was governor of both Polmont and Greenock, roles that helped him understand the pressures faced by his officers daily.

Derek McGill is a classic case of working your way up through the ranks to the top in easy stages. He started as an officer in Dumfries Young Offenders Institute in the seventies. Now at the pinnacle of his profession he likes to lead from the front rather than manage from behind a desk. He has a particular interest in the use and benefits of arts, drama, and music in a prison setting. One of his current ploys is to work with Theatre Nemo in starting up a prison choir. It is interesting that earlier in this book I spelled out the value of drumming in particular to youngsters incarcerated in the bleak halls of Scotland's great prisons. Derek himself, though no Gene Krupa, has played in groups in his youth and still enjoys laying a beat in behind any guys taking guitar lessons from prison volunteers.

Like Bill McKinlay he is aware of the physical limitations of the old gaol but rather than tear it down he would rebuild on the site. He points out the advantages – Barlinnie is near the busiest courts in the land, the prisoners are used to it and it is strategically placed for visitors. This is not an impossible task, a new prison building could be constructed in the current workshop and sports area and when finished the old buildings could be knocked down and that area used for library, class-rooms, sports ground etc. Bill McKinlay and Derek McGill share one bee in their respective bonnets. The constant tabloid harping on about prisoners enjoying the life of Riley with flat screen TVs etc. Derek points out the prisoners pay a tenth of their prison wages for the chance of a peek at a wee screen. How many on the outside would pay a tenth of THEIR wages for a telly! Another upside is that the tellies in the cells can be used to screen DVDs on subjects like suicide prevention. A down side he has noted is that the library is less used in the TV era.

Being in a prison daily inevitably makes you think about how the inmates got there and how you can prevent them coming back. Derek feels much of the blame for our high prison popu-lations lies with forces outside of the walls. He believes a high proportion of inmates have not been taught by the education system or their families how to face up to their problems. Instead they take the easy way out – thieving, drinking or drug taking. When inside the staff are encouraged to show inmates this side of their problems and encourage them to adopt a more positive attitude, to help them acknowledge why they are behind bars and how they could have avoided it. To get them to face up to their demons rather than run away from them.

A simple thing like a game of cards could help. The boredom of Barlinnie has recently been relieved a little by the reintro-duction of the old prison card game Bella. A pack without cards 2, 3 and 4 is used and it is a sort of combination of Whist and

Bridge. Bridge itself would no doubt be regarded as too poncy and suburban by the cons, but Bella, like it, is a game that requires concentration and deep thinking. It can encourage 'good mental health' as well as providing entertainment. Various tricks count for differing amounts of points and the duo with the highest total wins. One young inmate put his finger on a key benefit. It made me 'think tactically' he said. You also need to have a good head for figures and be able to work with your partner against an opposing couple. This game, sometimes the officers join in, passes many a long night but more than just killing time it goes a little way to educating prisoners in team play and thinking ahead, something many have never done. Las Vegas it isn't but Bella is enjoyed greatly by the cons and it encourages record keeping and mathematical skills. It would be overstretching it to say it is a trump card in the battle to make the penal regime work. But, as they say in the adverts, every little helps.

However the sad fact to be faced is that the optimism shown by concerned Glaswegians in the distant days of the eighteen eighties, in building Barlinnie, has not been fully rewarded. Problems and ongoing controversy still swirl, like the damp dark Glasgow winter mist, round the bleak prison. There are still too many challenges for comfort to be faced by the men and women who live behind the walls, on both sides of the bars. They walk a hard road. And will continue to do so.

BARLINNIE TIMELINE

1879 – Purchase of land for £9,750.

1882 – A-Hall commissioned.

1883 – B-Hall commissioned. Houses for chaplain and doctor built outside the walls.

1887 – C-Hall commissioned. Old Gate completed.

1888 – House for chaplain and doctor built outside the gate.

1889 – 35 'married wardens' quarters' built outside the prison.

1890 – Link corridor A, B, C halls built.

1892 – D-Hall commissioned.

1893 – Chapel completed. Perimeter extended to build E-Hall.

1896 – E-Hall completed.

1903 – Large workshop built. E-Hall altered to accommodate rise in short-term prisoners.

1908 – Old sheds built. Alterations to E-Hall.

1933 – Alterations to D-Hall to accommodate prisoners from Duke Street. New office block built adjacent to gate.

1939 – Gymnasium built. (Old) Library built.

1940 – Bread store and coal depot erected.

1949 – Handicraft workshop built.

1951 – Dining halls built (now psychology department, conference suite etc).

1954 – Old visits room completed.

1955 – Female block built due to closure of Duke Street. It later became the Special Unit.
1960 – Reception area reconstructed. Vocational training introduced.
1968 – New sheds completed.
1975 – Concrete modernization completed. Office complex completed. 'Arches' built on ends of halls.
1980 – New garage built.
1983 – Segregation unit completed.
1989 – Observation bridges built.
1997 – £5m refurbishment of D-Hall, including removal of gallows.
1999 – refurbishment of staff and visits area.
2002 – Slopping out ends. A, B and C Halls refurbished.
2004 – Work begins on E-Hall, ends 2005.
2007 – Entrance area refurbished.

GOVERNORS OF BARLINNIE PRISON

At the time of writing there have been 22 Governors
(J Taylor held the post twice, making 22 tours of duty):

Captain H Montieth:	15/08/1882 to 22/12/1882
J Taylor:	23/12/1882 to 03/09/1883
Major W Dodd:	04/09/1883 to 02/04/1888
J Taylor:	03/04/1888 to 31/07/1898
A Thompson:	01/08/1898 to 28/05/1908
J Cram:	01/06/1908 to 31/03/1914
WB Burglass:	06/05/1914 to 30/04/1927
Major RW Baird:	15/07/1927 to 01/04/1929
R Walkinshaw:	22/04/1929 to 11/01/1934
Captain J Murray:	09/02/1934 to 09/04/1935
W Findlayson OBE:	10/04/1935 to 30/04/1943
JP Mayo OBE:	04/05/1943 to 31/07/1954
JR Peddie MBE:	05/08/1954 to 05/08/1957
AH Anderson OBE:	05/08/1957 to 22/03/1964
D McKenzie ISO:	23/03/1964 to 17/11/1974
RF Hendry ISO:	28/11/1974 to 31/05/1979
AK Gallacher:	06/06/1979 to 01/07/1987
AR Walker:	02/07/1987 to 22/02/1990
P Withers:	23/02/1990 to 31/03/1995
R Houchin:	05/04/1995 to 30/08/2001
W McKinlay OBE:	01/09/2001 to 01/10/2011
D McGill:	04/10/2010 to ——————

INDEX